LIGHTHOUSES OF IRELAND

Roger O'Reilly, from Drogheda but now based in Kilkenny, is an award-winning artist and illustrator whose career has encompassed projects as diverse as storyboarding the *Vikings* TV series and illustrating for editorial and advertising clients around the world. His paintings are to be found in collections at home and abroad, including the Musée d'Histoire Contemporaine in Paris. In 2016, he launched the popular Irelandposters.ie, designing retro posters of Ireland in the style of the interwar railway advertisements. His lighthouse illustrations have grown from a small project illustrating a select few to a collection encompassing virtually all the lighthouses around our shores, estuaries and harbours.

The images in the book are available as prints from **IrelandPosters.ie**

Author's note: This book is not intended as a navigational aid. As light patterns and phases are liable to be changed at short notice, the author takes no responsibility for the accuracy of particular light patterns.

Visiting lighthouses

The vast majority of lighthouses are the property of and under the care of the Commissioners of Irish Lights, Harbour Road, Dun Laoghaire. Unless express permission has been granted, please do not enter beyond the perimeter walls. A number of lighthouses such as Hook Head, Mizen Head and Fanad Head are open to the public during tourist seasons and many more can be visited as guests through the Great Lighthouses of Ireland tourism initiative. A further number of lighthouses have open access days once or twice a year (see local papers for details).

Readers should note that this book is an information guide and does not act as an invitation to enter any of the properties or sites listed. No responsibility is accepted by the author or publisher for any loss, injury or inconvenience sustained by anyone as a result of using this book.

LIGHTHOUSES
OF IRELAND

An illustrated guide to the sentinels
that guard our coastline

Roger O'Reilly

The Collins Press

FIRST PUBLISHED IN 2018 BY
The Collins Press
West Link Park
Doughcloyne
Wilton
Cork
T12 N5EF
Ireland

Reprinted 2018

A CIP record for this book is available from the British Library.

Hardback ISBN: 978-1-84889-353-5

Design and typesetting by Anú Design, Tara
Typeset in Frutiger
Printed in Poland by by Białostockie Zakłady Graficzne SA

Images
P i: Rotten Island Lighthouse
P iii: Little Samphire Island Lighthouse

To Úna, the One,
and to the other three, Ellie, Katie and Rory

INISHTRAHULL

DUNREE   RATHLIN WEST   RATHLIN EAST
FANAD HEAD   RUE POINT
STROOVE
TORY ISLAND   MOVILLE

MAIDENS
BALLAGH ROCKS   CHAINE TOWER
ARRANMORE   FERRIS POINT
BLACKHEAD (ANTRIM
MEW ISLAND
RATHLIN O'BIRNE   ROTTEN ISLAND   DONAGHADEE
ST JOHN'S POINT
(DONEGAL)
METAL MAN   ANGUS ROCK
OYSTER ISLAND   ST JOHN'S POINT
EAGLE ISLAND   BROADHAVEN   BLACK ROCK (SLIGO)   (DOWN)

BLACKROCK (MAYO)   BLACKSOD   HAULBOWLINE
GREENORE
ACHILLBEG   DUNDALK
INISHGORT
CLARE ISLAND   TOWER OF LLOYD
DROGHEDA   DROGHEDA NORTH
DROGHEDA EAST &WEST
SLYNE HEAD   BALBRIGGAN
ROCKABILL
HOWTH
MUTTON ISLAND   NORTH WALL   BAILY
EERAGH   KISH
STRAW ISLAND   POOLBEG
INISHEER   DUN LAOGHAIRE WEST PIER
BLACK HEAD (CLARE)   DUN LAOGHAIRE EAST PIER   MUGLINS
WICKLOW HARBOUR
WICKLOW HEAD

SCATTERY ISLAND   BEEVES ROCK
LOOP HEAD
KILCREDAUN   TARBERT

ROSSLARE
LITTLE SAMPHIRE ISLAND   DUNCANNON   TUSKAR ROCK
INISHTEARAGHT   DUNMORE EAST   HOOK HEAD
DINGLE HARBOUR   BALLINACOURTY
VALENTIA   MINE HEAD
SPITBANK   YOUGHAL
SKELLIGS   BALLYCOTTON
ROCHES POINT
ARDNAKINNA   ROANCARRIG   CHARLES FORT
BULL ROCK   OLD HEAD OF KINSALE
SHEEP'S HEAD   BARRACK POINT   GALLEY HEAD
MIZEN HEAD   CROOKHAVEN
FASTNET

Contents

Foreword

As a keen yachtsman, I've long had a love of lighthouses and when I came across Roger's work through a friend at Newstalk Radio, I was immediately smitten. We met shortly afterwards when I had him as a guest on my show, coincidentally, shortly before I took up the position as chair of the Great Lighthouses of Ireland. When, a short while later, he asked me if I'd write a foreword to his new book, I didn't hesitate.

The working world of the lighthouse keeper and the heroic work carried out by the staff of the Commissioners of Irish Lights over the last 200 years in manning and maintaining the lighthouses, navigation buoys and beacons around our coast could be challenging and lonely work, with the beauty and drama of their locations scant compensation for such a tough life.

Technological progress has been a constant in maritime life and, when we look at its role in relation to lighthouses and the changing face of navigation, its effect has been especially marked. Over time, human intervention has been automated and whilst this results in a safer, more efficient and less costly service, we mourn the loss of the human touch as an aid and guide to our safety at sea. Starting with the replacement of the old lightships with Lanby automatic buoys, automation has resulted in the storytelling and tales of romantic nautical adventures being largely consigned to the history books.

While today lighthouses elicit different emotions than they did for past generations, they still capture the imagination in a way that few other structures in our built environment do. For those who prefer to keep their feet dry, they evoke a keen sense of the romance and adventure of life at sea and a reassuring benevolent presence when illuminated at night. For sailors, of course, they are a welcome first sight of safe harbour, while during daylight hours, they act as markers, beacons and, in the case of yacht races, destinations in themselves.

Lighthouses of Ireland takes us out and around our diverse coastline to explore the over 80 lighthouses that dot these shores. This visual tour also embraces the history of the lighthouses and records the endeavours of the great engineers, such as John Smeaton and John Richard Wighams, who made the technology possible, Belfast-born George Halpin, who coordinated the building of over 50 lighthouses in little over as many years, and innovators such the great French physicist Augustin Jean Fresnel, whose multipart lens was a game changer for maritime navigation. These buildings are testament to their acumen and their enterprise.

Roger has a unique gift. As an artist and a storyteller, his illustrations, coupled with his clear passion for lighthouses, results in a read where the beauty and history of these magnificent maritime temples is captured in a special and very unique way.

Bobby Kerr
Entrepreneur, broadcaster and Chair of Great Lighthouses of Ireland.
Great Lighthouses of Ireland is an all-island tourism initiative, developed by the Commissioners of Irish Lights,
featuring thirteen iconic sites in breathtaking coastal locations.
www.greatlighthouses.com

'I can think of no other edifice constructed by man as altruistic as a lighthouse. They were built only to serve.'

– George Bernard Shaw (1856–1950)

Introduction

There are over 80 lighthouses dotted around
Ireland's shores, varying in size from the colossus
that is Fastnet to more modest harbour lights. Their
architecture varies considerably, due mainly to the
demands of their location rather than to any design
trends of the day, as the vast majority were built
in the 57-year period between 1810 and 1867.
Lighthouses, in many ways, have no nationality and,
indeed, in times of war they are neutral, pledged
only to save life, to guide ships to shore and
away from rocky reefs, shoals and sandbanks.
As Europe's western outpost, our coastline's safety
is of immense importance to shipping plying the
Atlantic. The proliferation of lights that pepper
the coasts of Donegal and Antrim, of Kerry and
Cork, Waterford and Wexford reflect this concern
for safe passage into and out of European waters.
Storm battered and often inaccessible, the offshore
lighthouses of our western coast are of a different
mould from those along the east coast. A keeper's
three-week tenure on the likes of Eagle Island or
Inishtearaght could easily turn into a sojourn
double that length.

The collection of lighthouses contained here was
never meant to be comprehensive, but as time went
on, I ended up illustrating almost every substantial
light along our coastline and a good many estuary
lights while I was at it. Deciding where to start
this journey was a difficult decision. At our oldest
lighthouse? At our most dramatic? In the capital?
In the end, I decided to start where it began for me:
among the marram grass along the sand dunes that
define the southern shore of the Boyne estuary.

You might think that commencing with a clutch of
decommissioned estuary lights is an odd place to set
off on a journey celebrating our lighthouse heritage,
but in many ways, the North light at Drogheda, in an
age of rapidly changing technology, shines a light on
an optimistic and fruitful future for these structures.

The truth is that virtually all the lighthouses around
our shores are, in operational terms, already facing
redundancy. They are a backup system for when
a ship's GPS or navigational system fails or where
a vessel does not have the latest equipment. Even
in this role, they might often as easily be replaced
by an aluminium pole with an array of LEDs
– Roancarrig being a good example – were it not for
the great affection in which the public holds them,
a sentiment which the Commissioners of Irish Lights
appreciate. They are committed to preserving them
in as much as their remit allows, hence the Great
Lighthouses of Ireland initiative. At some stage in
the future, however, the Commissioners and local
councils will be forced to divest themselves of those
structures that cannot be repurposed and, in fact,
the process has begun, with a number of lighthouse
buildings being sold off as private dwellings and the
demolition of external buildings and storerooms at
many of the stations.

Drogheda North will be restored as part of the
Boyne tourist trail stretching from Mornington to
Newgrange, then onwards to Slane and eventually
Navan. It will preserve for the public this historic
structure and with it part of the legacy that
lighthouses have played in maritime history in this
country. Long may it shine!

I was a kid of the 1970s, growing up on the carefree beaches of east Meath at Bettystown. A short bicycle ride from our home was the Maiden Tower at Mornington. This 18-metre high tower was built during the reign of Queen Elizabeth I (hence the 'Maiden' in the name) and used as a beacon to aid ships navigating their way into the port of Drogheda. We would clamber up its spiral staircase to the platform at the top where we had a 360-degree view of the Boyne estuary, the distant town, the beaches stretching towards Skerries to the south and the Cooley Mountains to the north. We also had an enviable view of the shipping approaching the river mouth and it was easy to imagine what it must have been like 400 years ago, watching as merchant schooners and barques took bearings on the tower and cautiously navigated their way past the hazardous tides and currents and into the estuary. Four centuries later, the tower no longer served a purpose in guiding shipping to shore. It had been

superseded almost 100 years earlier by three unusual lighthouses situated among the dunes.

The north, east and west lights were truncated lighthouses that stood like daleks on stilts, gazing forlornly out to sea and only coming to life as dusk crept in and we reluctantly set our bikes towards home. The sense of peace and reassurance that I felt in the warm glow of those beacons as they ultimately illuminated the night has stayed with me ever since.

In 2015 I started a project – Irelandposters.ie – designing and illustrating retro posters of Ireland in the style of the old railway advertisements of the interwar years. The intention was to cover the 32 counties, the major towns and cities and whatever else inspired me along the way. It has been an ongoing and engaging project that fitted in alongside my main job of storyboarding and illustrating.

As an incentive to customers to buy a poster during the run-up to Christmas, I designed two lighthouse mini-posters – Fastnet and the Baily – which were included free with orders. It set the seed of an idea, which lay germinating until I had some spare time during the spring of 2016, when I got to illustrating some of the lighthouses on the south-east coast, near where I now live. I should have known it

The Maiden Tower at Mornington with Aleria beacon in the background.

wouldn't stop there. Before I knew it, I had decided to revisit the subjects of the original two posters and from there I was off on a journey illustrating all the lighthouses that dot our coastline.

Early on, I made the decision to exclude structures that did not fit the idea of a true lighthouse, i.e. if they had no living quarters or you couldn't physically go inside them, but as the project gathered pace I found myself unable to resist the charm of landmarks such as Angus Rock at Strangford Lough or the Muglins in Dalkey Sound. It would also have meant leaving out the signal station at

Mizen Head, which, while in operational terms is simply a light on a pillar, manages to occupy one of the most spectacular positions on our coastline. By the time it was complete, the project had gone on to encompass not just the coastal structures, but estuary and harbour lights too.

The earliest recorded lighthouses were built on the shores of upper Egypt. These navigational aids were often pyres built on the upper levels of monasteries or temples and attended to by priests or adherents who were also versed in the arts of seafaring.

As early as 247 BC, Alexander the Great's successor, King Ptolemy I, had commenced the construction of probably the greatest of all lighthouses and one of the wonders of the ancient world, the Pharos of Alexandria on the southern Mediterranean

coast. Incredibly, this structure, which took twelve years to build, survived a millennium and a half of storms, tides and war, eventually succumbing to an earthquake as late as the thirteenth century.

Our own pharological history is not quite so spectacular but no less interesting for that. In the fifth century St Dúbhan established a beacon on the headland then known as Hy Kinsellagh and now called Hook Head. The light would have been a brazier or metal cage of burning wood, turf or whatever he could lay his hands on, probably set on a small tower of stones, though there are also suggestions that he may have suspended the cage from a mast on the cliffs to warn approaching ships of the treacherous waters nearby.

William Marshall, Strongbow's son-in-law, subsequently established a permanent tower on the site in the thirteenth century. It is now the oldest operating lighthouse in these isles and the second oldest in the world (the Roman-era Tower of Hercules, near A Coruña in north-western Spain, is the oldest extant).

With the dissolution of the monasteries under Henry VIII, a valuable resource for safety at sea was removed in a stroke when the monks and priests were no longer there to look after these guiding lights. As a result of a petition put forward by a guild of Deptford-based mariners troubled by the poor conduct of unregulated pilots on the Thames, 'the Brethren of the most glorious and undivided Trinity, and of St Clement in the Parish of Deptford-Strond in the County of Kent' (Trinity House) was established in 1514 and tasked 'to make, erect, and set up such, and so many beacons, marks, and signs for the sea … whereby the dangers may be avoided and escaped, and ships the better come into their ports without peril'. Under Henry's successor,

Elizabeth I, there was official recognition of the importance of seamarks (hence the aforementioned Maiden Tower) and a law was established to punish anyone guilty of 'removal, alteration or defacement' of these structures or marks. The fine was £100 – quite an amount in those days (today that would be worth almost €75,000!).

Over the next 200 years a hotchpotch of systems of providing shore lights and markers existed in Ireland and England with no real regulation or oversight. Private franchisees and operators ran lighthouses that were often inefficient, poorly lit or sometimes simply not lit at all due to cost-cutting or negligence. In the 1830s, the keeper of Lowestoft Lighthouse, after lighting the lamp, would regularly lock up the building and head into town to ply his second trade as a waiter in nearby hostelries for 5 shillings a night. More worrying still was that, on occasion, keepers subcontracted their duties to others to make a little extra income. In one case a keeper hired an elderly woman who lived quite a distance from the lighthouse. In bad weather, when the light was most needed, she simply stayed at home. The situation was brought to a head only when a ship struck the rocks below the tower, with the loss of a costly cargo and all lives on board.

There was opposition, too, to the provision of lighthouses. The infamous 'wreckers' on the southern shores of these islands made profit from luring floundering ships towards the rocks with decoy beacons designed to send them to a watery end. Though the scale of this activity is probably exaggerated, they were in no hurry to see an organised system of lighthouses established along the south coast.

There was, however, such a confusion of chancers, speculators and the downright inept that, if further tragedies were to be averted, a body with the authority to regulate responsibility for the provision of navigational aids was urgently required and so, in 1836, Trinity House was vested with powers to buy out the last private lighthouse owners, and began refurbishing and upgrading its lighthouse estate. In 1786 under an Act of the Parliament for Ireland, the Commissioners of Irish Lights came into existence with responsibility for navigational aids around the coast of Ireland, both north and south. Today, their revenue is collected as light dues levied on all shipping that arrives in Irish ports, based on the net tonnage of the vessel, collected by the Customs Authority and then paid into a general lighthouse fund.

In the days before easy communications, to a ship on the final and perhaps most treacherous part of its voyage, the flash of the lighthouse would have signalled the end of a long journey and safe harbour for some well-earned respite. To present-day admirers, the lighthouse represents a unique part of our maritime history and an aesthetically pleasing part of our built heritage. However you might interpret it, at its core, a lighthouse is something far simpler: a tower and a beacon.

Long before GPS, radio transmission and radar, lighthouses served two primary purposes. The first was to guide shipping through waterways made treacherous by shoals, reefs and rocks as they left the open ocean and headed to port. Most lighthouses also included fog signals to warn ships of hazards during periods of low visibility.

The second purpose was to serve as a reference to mariners. An individual lighthouse distinguishes itself with its day mark – the colour schemes and patterns on the tower – and its light signature. For example, one flash every two seconds tells a sailor that they are near Valentia Island off the coast of Kerry. Four flashes every twenty seconds means that they are further north, approaching Loop Head in County Clare. Today, in the event of GPS failure, crews can still reference light lists to plot a course using lighthouses and their distinguishing traits.

From the start, the new body tasked with provisioning Ireland's lighthouses had to accommodate complex engineering systems and devices as well as a light-keeping staff to keep the lighthouses in perfect working order. In addition to a lighthouse, a complete light station might include a fog-signal building, living quarters for the keepers and their families, fuel stores and workshops. They also had to be at the forefront of new technologies affecting all aspects of navigational aid.

Early lighthouses used whatever materials were deemed suitable and available locally: wood, brick, stone,

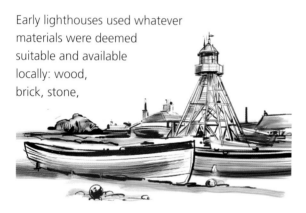

Lowestoft Low Lighthouse c. 1850.

concrete, and cast iron. The life of these early lighthouses was predictably short, especially if they were offshore. The rebuilding of the Eddystone Rock Lighthouse off Plymouth Sound on England's southern coast by the engineer John Smeaton set a milestone in the progression of lighthouse design. The difficulty of establishing any sort of building on the wave-swept rocks, particularly in the predominant swell, meant that despite their being a major hazard to shipping, all attempts at placing a warning on them had been decidedly temporary. Using granite blocks, Smeaton modelled the shape of his lighthouse on that of an oak tree. He pioneered the use of 'hydraulic lime,' a form of concrete that will set under water, and developed a technique of securing the granite blocks together

using dovetail joints and marble dowels. He also tapered the thickness of the tower towards the top, curving the tower inwards at a gentle gradient. This profile had the advantage of allowing some of the energy of the waves to dissipate on impact with the walls. This version of the Eddystone remained in use for over 100 years and the lessons learned were implemented in countless offshore lighthouses constructed over the next two centuries.

As mentioned earlier, the source of illumination for the ancient lighthouses had generally been coal, charcoal or wood. Vast quantities – in some cases as much as 400 tons per annum – were needed to keep these beacons burning. This was obviously expensive and extremely cumbersome to deliver and to manoeuvre on site. Subsequently, candles and oil lamps magnified by concave mirrors were experimented with as an alternative – with varying results. Smeaton's Eddystone was illuminated by 24 candles, for instance, and numerous other lighthouses adopted the technology, despite the light being rather feeble at best. The candles were made on site from tallow and each one would last a maximum of three hours.

With the invention in 1782 of the Argand lamp, with its steady smokeless flame, the technology of lighthouse illumination took a leap forward. The lamp had a sleeve-shaped candlewick mounted so that air could pass through the centre and around the outside of the wick before being drawn into a central chimney. It first used whale oil and later colza oil (rapeseed oil) as a cheaper alternative and became the standard for lighthouses for over a century.

Sometime later here in Ireland, John Richard Wigham pioneered a system of gas illumination for lighthouses. He was given a grant by the Dublin Ballast Board in 1865 and he fitted his new gas 'crocus' burner at the Baily Lighthouse on Howth Head, giving an output four times more powerful than the equivalent oil lights. An improved composite design, installed in the Baily light in 1868, was thirteen times more powerful than the most brilliant light then known.

In 1870, the light at Wicklow Head was fitted with Wigham's patent intermittent flashing mechanism, which timed the gas supply by means of clockwork. When this mechanism was combined with a

Five different lighthouses have been built on the Eddystone reef with varying degrees of success. The helideck was added above the lantern room to the current structure in 1980.

revolving lens in the Rockabill Lighthouse, the world's first lighthouse with a group flashing characteristic was produced.

In any industry at any given time, technologies shoot ahead in one quarter while they lag behind in others. The business of lighting our shores was no different. While the first electrically illuminated tower appeared in Dungeness in Kent as early as 1862, most lighthouses had to wait until the mid-twentieth century to convert to electricity and in some cases it happened as late as the 1970s.

With the arrival of the Argand lamp and its steady illumination, the development of optical lenses to increase and focus the light intensity got started in earnest. The first practical system used paraboloidal reflectors to concentrate the light into a beam, thereby making it visible from distances not previously achieved. The lens, however, was extremely heavy and expensive and, while numerous propositions for alternative lenses were put forward, the multipart Fresnel lens, developed in 1822 by the French engineer of that name, soon became the

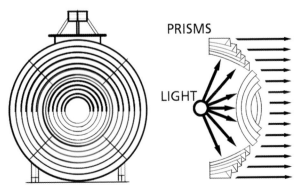

A Fresnel lens

standard fitting. His design allowed for lenses of large aperture and short focal length without the weight of glass that would be required of a conventional lens. It also projected the beam over longer distances.

The first Fresnel lens was fitted on the Cordouan Lighthouse on the western coast of France and could be seen from a distance of 32 kilometres. A beautiful example, which once graced the Baily Lighthouse, can be seen at the National Maritime Museum in Dun Laoghaire.

Ireland's golden age of lighthouse building came in the early nineteenth century. In 1800, when Francis Tunstall retired as Inspector of Works at the Dublin Ballast Board, he was succeeded by a Belfast man by the name of George Halpin. Halpin was just 21 years of age. His background was in construction rather than engineering, but he set to his new job with gusto. His position carried with it responsibility for the design, construction and maintenance of all

civil and mechanical works within Dublin Port, from Sutton on the north side of Dublin Bay to Bullock Harbour on the south. It included supervising the construction of new docks, bridges and a variety of other projects for the ever-expanding port. When the Ballast Board became responsible for lighthouses in 1810, Halpin was appointed Inspector of Lighthouses as well as Inspector of Works. At that time there were only fourteen lighthouses around the coast of Ireland. By the time the Ballast Board handed over responsibility for lighthouses to the Commissioners of Irish Lights in 1867 there were 72. Halpin designed and supervised the construction of a new lighthouse on average every fifteen months, resulting in over 50 additional lighthouses around the coast of Ireland in 57 years, including St John's Point in County Down, with its dizzyingly tall tower, Rathlin West Light, the upside-down lighthouse cut into the cliff face on Rathlin Island, the remote Skellig Michael Lighthouse and Fanad Head in Donegal, surely one of the most beautiful lighthouses in the world.

He also oversaw the modernisation of the original fourteen lighthouses.

When you visit these lighthouses, it is immediately apparent what a remarkable feat of engineering and construction they are. The workmanship and attention to detail, from the brasses and mosaics in the lantern rooms to the dovetail joints in the huge blocks of granite and Portland stone, speak of dedication and pride in the builder's craft.

George Halpin died suddenly in July 1854 at the age of 75, while carrying out an inspection of a lighthouse. He was succeeded by his son, George Halpin Junior.

The Anatomy of a lighthouse

The top of a lighthouse tower is where its most important function is performed. The lantern room is that portion of the top of the tower that encloses the lens. Generally this room is constructed of metal and glass and is a single- or double-storey structure mounted on the masonry tower. In the centre is the lens assembly, which can weigh several tons. It is supported on a bath of mercury, which keeps the lamp perfectly level and reduces friction so the whole arrangement can be rotated quite easily. These days the movement is powered by an electric motor, but originally it would have been operated by a clockwork mechanism using a weight running through a tube at the centre of the lighthouse tower. This was wound up half hourly and it regulated the speed at which the optic rotated.

The lantern room is surrounded by glass windows called storm panes. These are set into metal frames, whose vertical members are called astragals. Sometimes, as in Fastnet, the astragals are diagonal. Handholds are installed on the exterior of the astragals for the keeper to grip while standing on a ladder to clean the panes. These are accessed from the circular balcony or gallery that surrounds the lantern room.

Above the lantern is the cupola. The dome is made of metal and usually copper clad. It is surmounted by a ball vent, through which air can pass. The vent is topped by a lightning rod, and sometimes a wind vane to assist the keeper in discerning wind direction.

Below the lantern room is the watch room or service room, where the clockworks for rotating the optics are

Vent
Lantern
Balcony
Service Room
Lower Balcony
Lightkeeper's Bedroom
Kitchen
Principle Storeroom
Spare Bedroom for workmen or temporary inhabitants
Oil Room
Lower Store Room
Entrance Room
Water Tank
High Water – Spring
High Water – Neap

The Fastnet Lighthouse, County Cork.

positioned, along with various fuel tanks and vents. The service room is where the keeper cleaned the lamp chimneys, prepared the lantern for the coming night and stood watch. Since automation, these are unused.

Incandescent lights fuelled by vaporised paraffin were used in many lighthouses up until the early 1970s. Al Hamilton, a keeper on Rathlin East Lighthouse, related how in July 1969 he prepared the paraffin lamp and wound up the clockwork mechanism to keep the lens rotating, while in a corner of the room, he watched Neil Armstrong take his first steps on the moon on the black-and-white screen of his television.

On the offshore or 'rock' lighthouses as they were known, there were three keepers on duty sharing 6 four-hour shifts between them. The early morning watch started at 6 a.m. and ended at 10 a.m. The second was from 10 a.m. to 2 p.m. and so on. The keeper on the early 6–10 a.m. shift prepared the light for the day ahead. This entailed oiling up the light, cleaning the retort and getting the lantern ready for the evening. Breakfast would then be had by all and the relieving keeper would clean up the mess room and get everything shipshape.

Before the advent of electricity, the lens required a lot of care and attention, especially as the paraffin lamp fumes created a build-up of oily black residue on the glass of the optic. This would be cleaned using water and vinegar during the day, with one keeper on the inside and the other on the outside. Whoever was on the inside needed to keep moving around as the magnification of the lens was so powerful that on a sunny day it could seriously singe your clothes.

Delivering provisions on the relief run.

After it was shined and polished, linen curtains would be drawn over the lens to shield it from the sun. Since automation, the lens is allowed to revolve all day long so the sun does not build up heat in any one spot.

The keepers did a lot of routine work, such as polishing floors, painting and mending, alongside maintenance duties. Cooking was generally shared, though the divvying-up of cooking chores might depend on culinary skills and abilities. You ordered your groceries from the nearest town or village every

fortnight or so. The food was kept in deep freezes powered by paraffin oil, and later electricity, but fresh food was always a potential problem on the offshore postings. With bad weather you could be stranded on a rock for weeks before getting fresh eggs, milk or bread; emergency rations had to be considered with this in mind. Keepers often found themselves cutting away the rapidly encroaching mould in order to make the bread last a few extra days. Water was also at a premium and in the absence of a well was collected off the roofs. It was a finite commodity and was used for washing as well as drinking. The keepers was sure it had not been contaminated with seawater and would boil off a small amount in a pan to test it. If there was no telltale salt mark left behind, it would be regarded as fit to drink.

BUOYS : TYPES AND USES

Travelling around the coast or in and out of harbours, you will see a wide variety of buoys. Their forms and colours are varied and from a distance they can look quite small. When you get up close, however, or see them brought ashore for repair, you can appreciate just how big they actually are: some are as tall as a house. Shown above are the main types of buoy found along the Irish coast. Traditionally, conical buoys ('nuns'), with or without a painted top, always referred to starboard in a channel, while 'can' buoys, with a flat top, were port-hand buoys. Staffs and globes were used on starboard buoys, while staffs and cages were used on port-hand buoys. The silhouette of a buoy is important as the colour may not be apparent at a distance. On the cardinal buoys above, the two cones at the top indicate the direction it advises. Similarly, triangles, crosses and Xs help identify the marker when outlined against the horizon. At night, each buoy type has a distinctive light pattern, which helps sailors identify the marker.

Up until the 1940s an offshore posting meant being completely cut off from society until the end of your term, when, weather permitting, you could return to the mainland and your family. The arrival of radio telephones in the late 1940s was a boon as it meant that you could now communicate with other lighthouses, with ships and, on occasion, your nearest and dearest back on shore.

Ballydorn Lightship. Built in 1915 by the Dublin Dockyard Company for the Commissioners of Irish Lights, Ballydorn is a lightship with a hull of riveted iron and steel plate. It has two steel masts, used as steadying sails only.

ALF *Kittiwake*. Built in 1959, she is now in Dublin Port, awaiting a new life, possibly as a floating restaurant.

With advances in technology and especially in the area of remote monitoring in the 1960s and 1970s, it was inevitable that the business of navigational aids was going to move towards unmanned stations. The first part of the lighthouse estate to be automated were the lightships that dotted the east and south-east coasts in locations where the water was either too deep to build a lighthouse or where the ground was unsuitable, such as at the Kish Bank (about 11 kilometres east of Dublin). Until engineering advances in the 1960s resolved the problem of positioning a lighthouse on the sandbar, the Kish was patrolled by the lightship *Gannet*. (The first lightship in the British Isles dates back as far

as 1734 when the vessel *Nore* was placed near the mouth of the Thames.)

The ships were held in position using 3-ton mushroom anchors and displayed a light in a tall mast or tower. They usually also had a day marker, typically a large painted globe mounted on a rear mast. Life for the crew was uncomfortable and often dangerous as there are numerous instances of

The Lanby or Large Automatic Navigation BuoY was first used in the USA and adapted for use in Irish waters in the early 1970s.

lightships being sunk in fog by unwitting shipping. By the 1980s the lightships along Ireland's coast were being converted to Automatic Light Floats (ALFs) and were largely unmanned. The fate of these ships has not been a happy one, with many sold off for scrap and few retained in a preserved state. One notable exception is the former *Petrel*, now renamed the *Ballydorn* and preserved as the clubhouse of the Down Cruising Club in Strangford Lough.

The cost of running and repairing even unmanned lightships was substantial and, by the late 1960s, a potential replacement was being tested on the seas. The Lanby or Large Automatic Navigation BuoYs were intended to perform as a replacement for the lightships. The running costs were estimated to be as little as 10 per cent of those of a light-vessel and they were adapted for use in Irish waters in the early 1970s. They were constructed as a circular hull with a central light to provide all-round visibility, along with a foghorn and various antennae and beacons. It was planned that the navigation buoys would be monitored remotely and run for extended periods without repair. They proved unreliable, however, in rough seas and it proved difficult for staff to maintain and repair them as, even in a light swell, they would rotate on one axis while pitching on another, making concentrating (and avoiding severe sea sickness) almost impossible.

In late summer 2010 the last of the Lanbys was towed by the tender ILV *Granuaile* to the Coal Quay in Dublin Port and hoisted out of the water. It was replaced with a Type 1 buoy to mark the Codling Bank off Arklow. The new aids-to-navigation buoy has a focal plane in excess of 5 metres and is fitted with a racon and Automatic Identification System (AIS) and is a fraction of the size of its big brother. Thus ended the long tradition of major floating aids to navigation in Irish waters.

As an island nation, Ireland is dependent on maritime trade. A total of 95 per cent of our imports and exports arrive or leave aboard vessels, which in turn depend on navigational aids of various sorts to ensure their safe passage. The Commissioners of Irish Lights (CIL) are tasked with the management of all lights, buoys and beacons around our coast and with providing mariners with communications and data services. This information is used by all sorts of seafarers, from cargo ships to passenger vessels and ferries, from trawlers to the smallest leisure craft. Today, GPS, radar and radio have revolutionised the technology of marine pilotage, but lighthouses are still a vital part of the network of navigation aids to ships in Irish waters. Since the final lighthouse was automated in 1997, the Baily Lighthouse at Howth, all the work of keeping our lighthouses functioning is done remotely. The sentinels are no longer manned, but are monitored and controlled by technicians on screen, often many miles away.

Today's lighthouse staff have an array of technology, which gives constantly updated information on the operations of all the lighthouses and their associated equipment, ensuring they continue to provide illumination and guidance to sailors and continue a tradition of duty stretching back to St Dúbhan and his lonely vigil on Hy Kinsellagh, all those centuries ago.

Terms and abbreviations used in the book

Elevation:	The height above high water of the light. Given in metres.
Character:	The pattern of flashes distinct to a particular lighthouse plus the colour of the light.

Fl:	Flashing
Gr fl:	Group flashing
Iso:	Isophase, i.e. intervals of light and dark are the same
Oc:	Occulting, i.e. the intervals of light are longer than those of dark
Q:	Quick flashing
s:	Seconds
Colours:	G: green; R: red; W: white

As an example; Fl W 10s means flashing white once every ten seconds.

Catoptric:	Refers to the reflection of light. Mirrors are used to focus and magnify the lighthouse beam.
Catadioptric lens:	A lens that uses both a lens (dioptrics) and curved mirrors (catoptrics) to combine refraction and reflection in the focusing process.
Dioptric:	Refers to the refraction of light. Where the lens is convex, it is referred to as a dioptric lens.
Leading lights:	A pair of lights separated by a distance and which indicate safe passage for vessels navigating a shallow or dangerous channel. When viewed from the vessel, the lights should align, signalling that the right approach to enter the channel is being taken.
Relieving Station:	A rock station on which the keepers served a term, typically three weeks, but sometimes longer, before being relieved.

THE LIGHTHOUSES

Drogheda North Light

Inactive since 2000
Location: 53° 43' 26.7" N, 6° 15' 16.8" W
Elevation: 7m

On the lookout for breakfast.

In among the sand dunes, in the grounds of a private house, sits Drogheda North light, one of three sister lights built to guide ships past the treacherous sandbanks at the mouth of the River Boyne. A light station was established here in 1842 but this light and its two colleagues date from the 1880s. All three were decommissioned in 2000, and a restoration programme by the Drogheda Port Authority to bring the light back to its former glory is planned. The structure rests on intricately intertwined cast-iron supports with a ladder leading up to the lantern itself, which has glazed panels. The light is set within boundary walls that also enclose the original lighthouse keeper's house. For years, the lantern had a fixed light pattern, but when the Drogheda North light was eventually connected to

the electricity network back in the 1950s, the signal was changed to a flashing warning. Three years later, the Drogheda North light was changed again, to flashing red, while Drogheda West and East lights kept white signals.

In time, the North light (and hopefully also the East and West lights) will form a perfect example of old lighthouse technology, long since obsolete, but fitting in well with other restored sea-safety features in the area, such as the beacons and the old lifeboat house. When restoration work on the Drogheda North Light is completed, it will become part of the Boyne tourist trail. It will be open to the public for a number of days each year and for educational school trips.

A Drogheda Port Authority tugboat passes the Aleria light and marker at the mouth of the Boyne.

Drogheda East and West

Inactive since 2000
Location: 53° 43' 20.6" N, 6° 15' 12.4" W
Elevation: West Light: 8m; East Light: 7m

Like two alien craft from a H.G. Wells novel left stranded on the sand dunes, the East and West lights at Mornington stand sentinel over approaching shipping at the mouth of the Boyne. Before the present causeway was built, the sands at the mouth of the river created a bar that drifted north or south with the currents and tide, posing a hazard to shipping. Designed as a set of leading lights, these beacons were mounted on rails and could be realigned as the sandbar moved position. Once a ship had the two lights lined up, it knew it was on a true course to avoid running aground.

Fishermen's boats lie in the tall grass of the Boyne estuary embankment.

After 150 years, the East and West lights still stand majestic among the sand dunes at Mornington. All three, including the North light, were decommissioned in 2000. A trip to view the lights at Mornington is recommended. After checking out the lights – and please remember, they are on private property – and exploring the Maiden Tower and the Lady's Finger monument, you can finish with a brisk walk upstream along the river towards the estuary flats or southwards along the wide, bleached sands towards Bettystown.

A heron plies his trade.

Balbriggan

Location: 53° 36'46.8" N, 6° 10'42.6" W
Elevation: 12m
Character: Fl (3) RWG 20s
Range: W: 24km; R and G: 18km

Balbriggan is Ireland's second oldest active lighthouse, after Hook Head. In 1762 Baron George Hamilton had a limestone pier constructed and the lighthouse was added in 1769.

From here, corn and timber were shipped to Liverpool and beyond. The lighthouse was classified as a sea light until in 1860 the newly established Rockabill Lighthouse relegated it to the status of harbour light. By the 1960s, corrosion had damaged the dome beyond repair, and the decision was taken to remove it. The fixed light was replaced by a flashing unit mounted on a column.

Boats lie at low tide in Balbriggan Harbour while in the background a Dublin-bound train traverses the handsome eleven-arch viaduct, which dates from 1843/44.

Plans have been afoot for many years to replace the dome and to renovate the lighthouse and adjoining bathhouse. In early 2017, the plans were put on view. Hopefully, in the near future we will see the lighthouse's crown finally restored.

The sweep of beach and rock pools to the north of Balbriggan Harbour.

BALBRIGGAN
LIGHTHOUSE

BALBRIGGAN
COUNTY DUBLIN

Rockabill

Location:	53° 35' 48.7" N, 6° 00' 17.8" W
Elevation:	45m
Character:	Fl WR 12s
Range:	W: 33km; R: 26km

In 1837 the Drogheda Harbour Commissioners proposed that a lighthouse be built on Rockabill off the coast of Skerries, stating that the shipping, which frequented Drogheda, would cheerfully pay a toll towards a light on the island! The lighthouse tower was built between the years 1855 and 1860. It is composed of granite quarried from the Mourne Mountains in County Down and limestone from nearby Milverton. The name derives from the Irish *Carraig Dá Bheola*, meaning 'Two Lips Rock'. The lighthouse was automated on 1 April 1989 and the keepers were withdrawn. Thereafter, the station was put in the care of a part-time attendant.

The Roseate Tern is found in only two main colonies in Ireland, one on Rockabill, and one at Lady's Island, in County Wexford. They are a rare summer visitor, arriving in April and staying until October.

During the summer months, Skerries Sea Tours run a daily passenger trip to the lighthouse.

The island is home to a colony of Roseate Terns, amongst the continent's rarest breeding seabirds, which, during the season, can be very protective of their young and have been known to dive-bomb keepers and visiting technicians whom they deem to be getting too close to their nests.

The Skerries Coast Guard crew during a training exercise, with Shenick Island (right) and Rockabill in the background.

Howth

Inactive since 1982
Location: 53° 23' 36.1" N, 6° 04' 00.6" W
Elevation: 17m

At the beginning of the nineteenth century, the decision was made to construct a new harbour at Howth to handle the steam-packet mail from Holyhead, thus replacing the old landing point at Pigeon House on the south of Dublin Bay.

Prior to this, the makeshift quays had been used mainly by local fishermen and as a fuel-offloading depot for the lighthouse further up on the headland.

The harbour's shortcomings, however, quickly became apparent as the channels rapidly silted up and it was only with tremendous effort that sufficient depth could be maintained for the new traffic. Within a few short years, construction had started on a more suitable alternative at the other side of Dublin Bay in Dun Laoghaire.

Gannets and guillemots patrol the island of Ireland's Eye, a short ferry ride from Howth Harbour.

The construction of the harbour lighthouse got under way in 1817, while the building of the adjoining Georgian-style residence had to wait for a further four years. We can only assume that the keeper must have lived during the interval in the cramped confines of the tower, as he would have been required to be on duty at all times. The buildings were also intended for defensive purposes: the strong circular wall defended a gun position.

It was here at Howth that Erskine Childers famously landed arms for the Irish Volunteers from his yacht, the *Asgard*, in July 1914. He was later executed by the authorities of the Irish Free State during the Civil War. His son, Erskine Hamilton Childers, went on to become the fourth President of Ireland in 1973.

The old tower light was decommissioned in 1982 when the harbour was modernised and the replacement light on the east pier was established.

Founded as Howth Sailing Club in 1895, the redesigned clubhouse of Howth Yacht Club sits like a candy-striped confection on the middle pier of the village's harbour.

HOWTH
LIGHTHOUSE

HOWTH HARBOUR
COUNTY DUBLIN

Baily

Location: 53° 21' 41.5" N, 6° 03' 09.5" W
Elevation: 41m
Character: Fl W 15s. Exhibited by day in
                poor visibility
Range: 33km

The first lighthouse at Howth Head was built in about 1667 by Sir Robert Reading, and was one of six for which Reading had received letters of patent to build from Charles II.

The original compound was higher up on the hill and comprised a small cottage with a square tower on its eastern side, which supported a coal-fired beacon. This lighthouse was known as the 'Green Bayly' and in 1912 archaeologists uncovered parts

Kittiwakes nest on Howth's cliffs.

of the original building. As technology advanced, the Port Authority of Dublin hired Thomas Rogers, with a view to improving the light. Rogers had invented a new catadioptric light, which used six Argand lamps, each with a silvered copper parabolic reflector that focused the light through six bullseye lenses to give a vastly improved light beam towards the sea. The new mechanism was erected on the same site but it soon became obvious that the site was too high. Constantly lost in mist, the light was further compromised by the fact that Rogers, now in the employ of the Revenue Commissioners and in complete control of the lighthouse, hired too few keepers and paid them too little. The keepers resorted to a plethora of odd jobs to supplement their meagre wages, including the building of an illegal distillery. Eventually, the management of lighthouses was taken back from the Revenue Commissioners and awarded to the Port Authority, which issued a recommendation that the lighthouse be moved south along the headland to Little Baily, or Dungriffin. A new tower and house for the keeper, designed by George Halpin Senior, the corporation's Inspector of Works, was completed in 1814.

In late 1996, the lighthouse was converted to automatic operation, and the last of the keepers left on 24 March 1997, making the Baily the last Irish lighthouse to be automated.

On the cliff walk from Sutton, heading north, with the Baily Lighthouse in the background.

THE BAILY
LIGHTHOUSE

HOWTH
COUNTY DUBLIN

North Wall

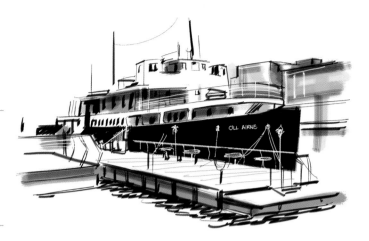

Location:	53° 20′ 44.5″ N, 6° 12′ 59.9″ W
Elevation:	12m
Character:	Fl 2s, 0.2s flash 1.8s eclipse, W
Range:	18km

The renovated training vessel MV *Cill Airne*, berthed on the North Wall, now has a second life as a chic restaurant and bar.

In the early eighteenth century, Dublin had a thriving trade with ports throughout Britain and beyond, exporting linen and agricultural goods and importing wine, coal and luxury items for the great Georgian houses of Ireland. The shipping channel in Dublin Bay, however, was too shallow for larger vessels and ships were often forced to unload their cargo at Ringsend and transfer to smaller vessels, or 'lighters', that could safely travel upriver.

Until 1800, most of the trade took place on the south side of the River Liffey, but with the opening of the new Custom House in 1791, port development shifted across to the north bank.

The original Custom House Dock opened in 1796 and it was followed in 1821 by George's Dock, providing a vastly increased area of warehousing and storage vaults. These formed part of the new Custom House Dock Area. At this time, the original

harbour light at the North Wall was constructed, to guide shipping upstream to the landing stages.

In 1836 construction work began on deep-water berths at the North Wall and these were extended in the 1870s. Further deep-water berths, in the Alexandra Basin, opened shortly before the First World War. In 1904 at the basin's entrance, the present 12-metre-high lighthouse was completed, to replace its predecessor, and is painted black with two white bands. The lighthouse is operated by the Dublin Port Company, which also operates two tugboats: the *Beaufort*, named after Sir Francis Beaufort, who created the scale of measurement for wind force in use worldwide today. The other, pictured here, is the *Shackleton*, named for Sir Ernest, the Kildare-born Antarctic explorer.

One of the two sets of Scherzer rolling lift bridges along Dublin's North Wall. Built in 1911, they allowed access for water traffic to the basins along the quay.

NORTH WALL
LIGHTHOUSE

NORTH WALL DOCKS
COUNTY DUBLIN

Poolbeg

Location: 53° 20' 31.8" N, 6° 09' 04.7" W
Elevation: 20m
Character: R 8s on, 4s off, 4s on, 4s off
Range: 31km

Sanderlings forage along the shoreline.

Dublin Bay in the seventeenth century was wild, open and exposed to every gale and wind. Ships frequently had to seek shelter at Clontarf to the north of the city or at Ringsend in the south. In stormy conditions, vessels often could not reach the city for several weeks at a time and shipwrecks were common. In 1716 the Ballast Office Committee started work on building a bank to protect the south side of the channel at the mouth of the harbour, running from Ringsend to Poolbeg.

The 'piles' as the bank was known, provided only limited protection from the worst of the weather and in 1753, after a particularly vicious winter, the bank was replaced with a wall – the South Bull Wall.

The Poolbeg Lighthouse at the end of the Bull Wall was lit for the first time on 29 September 1767. It replaced a floating light that had been maintained at the end of the wall to warn ships.

At the time, Poolbeg Lighthouse looked quite different from how it appears today, being shorter and tapering in at the top. It was crowned by an octagonal lamp, reached from the inside by a spiral staircase.

Poolbeg constitutes one of a formation of three lights that guide shipping through the bay. The others are the North Bull on the opposite bank ('Bull' being another word for strand or bank) and the other is on a wooden platform mid-channel. The lighthouse is painted red to indicate port side when entering the channel, while the North Bull is coloured green for starboard.

On a historical note, the low-water mark of the spring tide on 8 April 1837 at Poolbeg was used by Ordnance Survey Ireland as a standard height for all its maps, until that tradition was discontinued in 1958.

Poolbeg Lighthouse is now fully automated and is managed by Dublin Port Company.

Poolbeg Lighthouse from the sea, with the twin chimneys of the Pigeon House in the background.

Kish

Location: 53° 18' 39.0" N, 5° 55' 32.5" W
Elevation: 29m
Character: Fl (2) 20s, 24-hour light
Range: 40km

The Kish Bank is a shallow sandbank about 11 kilometres off the coast of Dublin. Until the present lighthouse was installed in 1965, the bank had been signalled by various lightships dating back as far as 1811. In foggy weather the ship would sound a gong, but when the Holyhead packet was expected, an 18-pounder gun was fired. An attempt was made to build a lighthouse here using screw piles, invented by Alexander Mitchell in 1842, but it was abandoned when the building was destroyed by severe weather. Lightships of various sorts were used right up until the last of these, the *Gannet* was withdrawn after the establishment of the new lighthouse.

The cup awarded to the winners of the gruelling 25km Hobblers Challenge rowing race from Dun Laoghaire out around the Kish and back.

In 1960 the Commissioners of Irish Lights investigated the possibility of erecting a platform similar to an oil rig. This would, however, be a reinforced concrete lighthouse with helicopter landing pad on top, rather than a steel structure. Design proposals were invited and the contract was eventually awarded to the Danish company Christiani & Nielsen. The lighthouse was built at the Coal Harbour in Dun Laoghaire. The first section of lighthouse cracked while it was being built and had to be discarded. It ended up forming part of the outer harbour wall at Greystones.

The second telescopic lighthouse was successfully completed and towed to its position in July 1965, where it was extended to its full height of 30 metres, with a projected lifespan of 75 years.

For just over a quarter century the white tower, with its distinctive red band and topped off with a helicopter pad, was manned by a crew of three. The tower is a self-contained unit of twelve floors, which includes keepers' quarters, storage, a generator, radio equipment and, of course, the lantern.

Crew were transferred in rough weather to the lighthouse by being winched in a cradle pod from the lighthouse tender ship. In 1992, the lighthouse was automated and the keepers withdrawn, ending another chapter in the history of Irish lighthouses.

The old Kish lightship, which guided vessels away from the banks until being retired with the establishment of the lighthouse.

KISH BANK
LIGHTHOUSE

DUBLIN BAY
COUNTY DUBLIN

Dun Laoghaire West Pier

Location: 53° 18' 11.4" N, 6° 07' 51.6" W
Elevation: 11m
Character: Fl (2) G 7.5s
Range: 13km

The tower of the old *Kittiwake* lightship

The quieter (and longer) West Pier at Dun Laoghaire was constructed between 1820 and 1827 and measures 1,548 metres. Between them, the West and East piers shelter one of the largest and most developed marinas in Ireland. Besides the shipping that plies the routes between Britain and Ireland, the marina is home to over 800 berths for visiting seafaring vessels of all shapes and sizes. Dun Laoghaire also plays host to four outstanding yacht clubs, the Royal Irish, founded in 1831, the Royal St George, founded in 1838, the National, established in 1871 and the more recent Dun Laoghaire Motor Yacht Club, founded in 1965.

The harbour and surrounding promenade is also a very popular destination for walkers, joggers and day trippers who come to take in the sea air, enjoy the scenery and if the sun is out, sample an ice-cream cone or a cool drink.

The lighthouse on the West Pier was established in 1852, five years after its sibling across the harbour entrance. The metalwork is painted green, indicating starboard for vessels entering the harbour.

When the East Pier Lighthouse was made into a three-keeper light, the principal keeper and his family moved out to the spartan but presumably superior comfort of the house on the West Pier. This would have entailed a daily commute of rowing a boat the short distance across the harbour entrance, unless the weather was foul, in which case he would have had to take a considerable detour into town and back out the opposite pier.

The lighthouse was automated as far back as 1930 with its fixed red light changing to three red flashes every ten and latterly every seven and a half seconds.

The headquarters of the Commissioners of Irish Lights at Dun Laoghaire. In the foreground is one of the modern cardinal buoys, which are quickly revolutionising navigational aids at sea.

Dun Laoghaire East Pier

Location: 53° 18' 09.0" N, 6° 07' 37.8" W
Elevation: 17m
Character: Fl (2) R 10s
Range: 31km

During the six years that it took to complete the East Pier, from 1817 to 1823, a wooden beacon was positioned at its extremity to warn shipping of danger, and as the pier progressed, the beacon moved with it. By the mid-1840s plans were at an advanced stage for a permanent light on the causeway and in October 1847 the light was established, belting out 12,000 units of candlepower at a height of 12.5 metres above high water.

Only 30 years later, the Commissioners of Irish Lights were being pressured to improve the power and range of the lights at Kingstown (as Dun Laoghaire was known at the time). In 1892, the City of Dublin Steam Packet Company, which had a monopoly on the Holyhead–Kingstown mail route, complained to the Commissioners of the poor harbour lighting.

Coffee and ice creams on the East Pier.

As a result, the tower on the East Pier was heightened by 3.6 metres and a new dioptric lighting system was installed, thus casting a beam on the Muglins rocks off Dalkey for the very first time.

The original fog bell had been replaced by a tall wooden belfry with a new bell, which in turn was succeeded by a reed horn, then the firing of a gun, a mechanised bell and finally a diaphone fog signal.

The lighthouse is surrounded by a defensive battery, but its military service has been uneventful. Its main historical role has been as one of only two stages in the state for the firing of gun salutes (the other being Spike island in Cork).

In July 1968 the East Pier station switched from vaporised paraffin to electricity for its lantern, and became unmanned. The new candlepower was 226,000 units, twenty times the power of its original light.

The upside-down fog bell of the East Pier lighthouse.

EAST PIER
LIGHTHOUSE

DUN LAOGHAIRE
COUNTY DUBLIN

Muglins

Location: 53° 16' 31.4" N, 6° 04' 33.3" W
Elevation: 14m
Character: Fl R 5s
Range: 20km

Just a few hundred metres off Sorrento Point on Dublin's south coast sits Dalkey Island with its Martello tower, St Begnet's Church and a herd of wild goats. The three small islands to the north are Lamb Island, Clare Island and Maiden Rock; to the north-east are the rocks and islands that comprise the Muglins.

Populated by seagulls, shags and cormorants, over the years these rocks have seen their share of shipwrecks and, in 1873, following the loss of a over a dozen ships off the island, the slow wheels of change were set in motion. After a slew of recommendations and seven years of further shipwrecks, a stone conical tower, 9 metres in height, was constructed as a day mark on the shoals. It was initially painted white; the red band was added later as an additional visual mark.

The Muglins' Martello tower and its famous inhabitants bask in the afternoon sun.

In the intervening period, the East Pier lighthouse at Dun Laoghaire – or Kingstown as it was then known – had been raised up by 3.6 metres, illuminating the rocks at night and thus providing some paltry assistance to skippers trying to navigate the rocks. Eventually, in June 1906, a light was finally established on the beacon, using oil gas as its fuel. In 1997 the Muglins Lighthouse was converted to solar-powered electric light and its range was increased to 20 kilometres.

Saint Begnet's church on Dalkey Island.

THE MUGLINS
LIGHTHOUSE

DALKEY SOUND
COUNTY DUBLIN

Wicklow Harbour

Location: 52° 58' 59.3" N, 6° 02' 03.8" W
Elevation: 11m
Character: Fl WR 5s
Range: 11km

Built in 1884 and operated by the Wicklow Port Authority, Wicklow East Pier Lighthouse is actually at the southern end of the harbour. It is an early example of mass concrete construction, which, while built at the *fin de siècle*, seems to have more of an art deco quality, with its simple cantilevered gallery and unadorned front entrance.

The name Wicklow is derived from the Norse *Wykylo* meaning 'Viking's Loch'. The Broad Lough feeding into the Leitrim River is separated from the Irish Sea by a narrow area of land known as the Murrough, an ancient Gaelic word meaning 'sea warrior', possibly with reference to Wicklow's history as a Viking stronghold. Being tidal, with a mixture of fresh and

A sorry-looking capstan along the quays. These were used to haul boats inshore against the tide.

brackish water, this relatively small area attracts a wealth of birdlife, such as black-headed gulls, great black-backed gulls, herring gulls, grey herons, little egrets, cormorants, shags, kingfishers and mute swans, while the water life has on occasion included basking sharks entering the harbour to feed on plankton at the mouth of the river.

Now overlooking the harbour, but originally mounted on a gun carriage, this was one of a number of cannon deployed along the coast to protect against a possible French invasion.

Wicklow Head

Location: 52° 57' 55.2" N, 5° 59' 53.3" W
Elevation: 37m
Character: Fl (3) W 15s
Range: 43km

Seals sunning themselves at a beach near Wicklow Head.

Back in 1781, it was decided to build two octagonal lighthouses on Wicklow Head, the most easterly point in the Republic. The two lights were established to mark the headland but also to distinguish it from Howth and Hook Head, which had only one light apiece. By lining up the two lights, ship's masters also had a lead west by north-west between the treacherous India sandbank and the Arklow Bank.

The rear or higher of the two original towers survives to this day. The front tower was demolished as part of the next development, which led to the construction of the 'new' Wicklow Head Lighthouse illustrated at right.

The old octagonal tower at Wicklow Head.

While the plan to place a beacon as high as possible on the headland to cast light far and wide appears sound, fog has a tendency to obscure the realisation of that vision. It was quickly concluded that the lights would need to be situated lower on the promontory and so, in 1818, the new lighthouse was established on the cliff edge as a front light while a new rear tower was erected near the site of the old lower tower.

Confused? We're not finished yet!

In the meantime, the old upper tower remained in place as a landmark, but was struck by lightning and caught fire, rendering it uninhabitable. The chief engineer, George Halpin, recommended that it be capped with a brick dome as soon as possible to preserve it and with all due haste; this was completed 30 years later.

In 1865 a new light vessel, the *Wicklow Swash* rendered the new rear tower obsolete and was itself withdrawn two years later when lightships were established at the Codling Banks and North Arklow.

In spring 1994, the lighthouse was converted to automatic operation and the keepers were withdrawn from the station. The rear octagonal tower survives today under the care of the Landmark trust and is now available as holiday accommodation as part of the Great Lighthouses of Ireland initiative.

WICKLOW HEAD
LIGHTHOUSE

DUNBAR HEAD
COUNTY WICKLOW

Rosslare

Location: 52° 15' 25.8" N, 6° 20' 16.8" W
Elevation: 15m
Character: Fl WRG 5s
Range: W: 28km; R and G: 18km

Motorcyclists taking part in a
rally disembark from the ferry.

The first lighthouse recorded at Rosslare port dates back to 1886, although no record of its appearance survives. The present lighthouse dates from 1906 when the new pier was built to facilitate the larger ferries crossing to the south Wales coast and later to France.

The origins of Rosslare as a cross-channel ferry port began more than century ago in 1898, when a joint Act of Parliament established the Fishguard & Rosslare Railways and Harbours Company to provide a service from London to southern Ireland.

After the visit of Queen Victoria to Killarney in 1861, it became a popular tourist attraction and as soon as it was feasible, railway companies operated excursions from London to Killarney, travelling out

An old cannon on the coastal path
at Rosslare Harbour, County Wexford.

overnight on a Friday and returning that weekend on an express train to the port. The new company was tasked with constructing facilities at Fishguard and Rosslare, as well as establishing a direct railway link between Rosslare Harbour and Cork.

The route officially opened in the summer of 1906 when a special train conveyed the Viceroy, Lord Aberdeen, and other dignitaries from Dublin's Kingsbridge Station (now Heuston) to Waterford and then over the new route, while the Great Western Railway operated one of the new steamers from Fishguard to the official opening. The route still survives despite the changing transport scene from when the first sailings began in 1906.

The lighthouse itself is an iron-framed circular construction enveloped in metal sheeting and it perches like a toy lantern at the end of the harbour wall. Due to security issues, it is no longer accessible to the public. The light shows white from the harbour, green from north and red when approaching from the south-east.

ROSSLARE
HARBOUR LIGHTHOUSE

ROSSLARE
COUNTY WEXFORD

Tuskar Rock

Location: 52° 12′ 10.5″ N, 6° 12′ 26.7″ W
Elevation: 33m
Character: Q (2) W 7.5s. Exhibited by day and
             by night
Range: 45km

Cormorants near Tuskar Rock.

Tuskar Rock Lighthouse stands 37 metres tall and is constructed from granite blocks. In October 1812, a ferocious storm struck the Wexford coast, and the swell swept away the temporary wooden barracks that had been erected on the island, drowning ten of the 24 workmen. The survivors were forced to cling to the rocks for 48 hours before being discovered and rescued. Two years later, a stonecutter fell to his death from the as-yet-incomplete tower. In June 1815 the lighthouse was finally completed and came into operation.

The name Tuskar comes from old Norse and simply means large (*tu*) rock (*skar*). While the Vikings, with their shallow-draught longboats, might have regarded the rock as a mere obstacle to be avoided, these shoals are believed to have caused more shipwrecks than any other site along the Irish shoreline.

In May 1859 the clipper *Pomona*, while en route from Liverpool to New York, floundered during high winds not far from Tuskar. By the time the Rosslare lifeboat arrived on the scene, only the mizzenmast

The Rosslare lifeboat on patrol exercises near the lighthouse.

was showing above the waves. The captain along with almost 400 of his passengers had perished. A scandal was to ensue when it was found that some of the bodies that had washed up on Ballyconigar beach had been looted.

During wartime, isolated rocks like Tuskar were very vulnerable to mines set adrift from their moorings. One of these mines exploded when it collided with the rock in December 1941, seriously injuring two assistant keepers, W.J. Cahill and Patrick Scanlan. They were both were brought ashore by the Rosslare lifeboat but unfortunately Scanlan did not survive his injuries.

While the isolation of a lighthouse can be restrictive, it can also open up unusual opportunities. In 1821 the two keepers on the rock were found guilty by the Ballast Board of aiding and abetting the smuggling of brandy, tea and silks from France. Their downfall had been partaking too liberally of the smuggled goods. It just so happened that in the middle of their reverie, the King of England, George IV, happened to be sailing past and remarked that the lights were not displayed. As a result of the subsequent investigation, principal keeper M. Wisheart was reduced to an assistant keeper, while assistant keeper C. Hunter was returned to his previous employment as a blacksmith in the Ballast Office's workshop.

Wisheart, although not found to be directly involved in the misdemeanour, was deemed to have abetted the operation. Some years later he fell to his death whilst cutting grass for his cow on Skellig Rock.

On 31 March 1993 the lighthouse was converted to automatic operation and the keepers were withdrawn from the station.

TUSKAR ROCK
LIGHTHOUSE

ROSSLARE
COUNTY WEXFORD

Hook Head

Location: 52° 07' 25.5" N, 6° 55' 46.4" W
Elevation: 46m
Character: Fl W 3s
Range: 43km

A seagull takes flight.

The present structure at Hook Head is about 800 years old and is the second oldest intact operational lighthouse in the world. It was founded by St Dúbhan, a Welsh monk who settled on the peninsula, then known as Hy Kinsellagh. Legend has it that, distressed at finding so many shipwrecked sailors washed up on the rocks below, he commissioned a local blacksmith to make a chauffer or metal basket, in which he built a fire and displayed it on the cliffs each night to warn ships away.

The present tower stands four storeys high, with walls up to 4 metres thick, and has three rib-vaulted medieval chambers in the lower tier. The ground floor served as a fuel store, while the second storey

At Hook Head you may come across an old starboard buoy and two anchor types: a kedge and a mushroom. The first was popular on ships and the latter was more suited for permanent moorings such as lightships.

of the lighthouse acted as the monastery. In later times this was converted into quarters for the assistant keeper, while the third floor was reserved for the principal keeper. The upper, narrower section in times past would have carried the warning beacon. The tower is constructed of local limestone and the original building survives intact. A total of 115 steps brings you up to the gallery, which has panoramic views of the surrounding countryside. In the seventeenth century, the lighthouse served as a centre for money counterfeiting. Its remoteness and the ease of spotting curious visitors approaching made it an ideal base for criminal activities. The lighthouse is also reputed to be the origin of the phrase, 'by hook or by crook'. Back in 1170, the Norman earl Strongbow landed here on his way to capture Waterford. He instructed his men to land by 'Hook or by Crooke' as the village of Crooke lay across the harbour from the lighthouse.

In 2001 the light was opened to the public as a tourist attraction after the old keepers' houses were turned into a visitor centre. Ten years later in January 2011, the Hook's mournful foghorn was heard for the last time as all remaining lighthouse foghorns were finally turned off.

Hook Head is one of twelve lighthouses that make up Great Lighthouses of Ireland, a new all-island tourism initiative, and is open to visitors year-round.

HOOK HEAD
LIGHTHOUSE

HOOK HEAD PENINSULA
COUNTY WEXFORD

Duncannon North

Inactive since 2006
Location: 52° 13' 44.3" N, 6° 56' 13.5" W
Elevation: 34m

Set high on a hill overlooking Waterford Harbour, Duncannon North Lighthouse or Duncannon North Rear Range Light, to give it its full name, is a rarity in Ireland in being a privately owned lighthouse that is still operational, although these days, the Port of Waterford, its guardians, use it only as a backup light.

Alongside its sibling at Duncannon Fort, the North Lighthouse formed a leading light to guide ships over the bar at Duncannon.

This is, in fact, the original lighthouse that stood at Roches Point in Cork. After 20 years of service it was deemed too small to accommodate a lantern big enough to maintain a strong light. Built in 1817, the lighthouse was dismantled block by block

A gun emplacement below the now defunct Duncannon Fort Light.

and in 1838 was shipped to Duncannon. It was then transported by horse and cart up the hill and reassembled in its present site.

The light was originally oil burning but was converted to acetylene in 1937 and to electricity in 1971. It was decommissioned in 1991 and temporarily recommissioned in 1996.

The Hooked Kitefest takes place on Duncannon beach each August.

DUNCANNON
LIGHTHOUSE

DUNCANNON
COUNTY WEXFORD

Dunmore East

Location: 52° 08' 56.1" N, 6° 59' 20.2" W
Elevation: 13m
Character: Fl WR 8s
Range: W: 31km; R: 24km

Sea kayaking is a popular activity along the Copper Coast.

In the early 1800s Dunmore was a sleepy fishing village best known for the bounty of herring shoals off Baginbun Bay at the onset of winter. In 1814 it was chosen by the Post Office to be the Irish terminal of a new mail packet route from Milford Haven in Wales. The Post Office engaged the Scottish engineer Alexander Nimmo to design and build a new harbour to accommodate the mail ships. His design included the elegant lighthouse, which takes the form of a fluted Doric column, with the lantern on top of the capital and a cast-iron lattice balcony below. The tower reaches a height of 13.5 metres above high water but because of the way it is integrated into the harbour wall, it seems much shorter from the seaward side. If you stand on that harbour wall and look south across the estuary of the Three Sisters (the Barrow, Nore and Suir), you

will see Hook Head Lighthouse and to its left, the spooky silhouette of Loftus Hall. The hall is said to be haunted by the Devil himself, alongside the ghost of a young lady, who was part of a group playing him at cards. He flew through the roof in a rage when his disguise was uncovered, she having spotted his cloven hooves beneath the card table. The poor lady lost her mind, while the identities of the other players and who exactly pocketed the winnings remain a mystery!

The 40 steps to the sea at Creadan Head on the Dunmore side of the estuary mark the end of an ancient Celtic route to the coast and the nearby Trá na mBan Gorm ('the strand of the blue women' – in Irish, 'black man' is a term preserved exclusively for the Devil, and hence dark skin is described as blue). The name is thought to have derived from the African slave trading that took place here, alongside general smuggling, in the eighteenth century. The path also passes the nearby Bronze Age tomb known as the Giant's Grave, which is believed to be over 4,000 years old.

The passenger and mail service to Dunmore from Milford Haven continued until 1835 when Waterford replaced it as the Irish terminal, thus avoiding a lengthy road journey out to Dunmore.

In 1903 the lighthouse was cleaned of the original whitewash and restored to its natural stone colour. In the mid-1960s, acetylene gave way to electricity and in August 1981 the optic lamp was converted to mains electricity.

The village of Dunmore East with its picturesque thatched cottages.

DUNMORE EAST
LIGHTHOUSE

DUNMORE EAST
COUNTY WATERFORD

Ballinacourty

Location: 52° 04' 41.3" N, 7° 33' 10.9" W
Elevation: 16m
Character: Fl (2) WRG 10s
Range: W: 18km; R and G: 15km

Perched on the low-lying rocky shore to the east of Dungarvan Bay, Ballinacourty Lighthouse was established, at the initiative of the merchants and shipowners of Dungarvan, to guide ships into the town. It was first exhibited in 1858 and stands 16 metres above sea level, the tower being constructed of local limestone.

By the late 1800s iron and steel had replaced wood as the favoured materials for building ships. These heavier, faster ships were valuable and the owners and the captain would be loath to abandon the vessel unless absolutely necessary. Off the Waterford coast at Ballinacourty, this was to prove fatal to the crew and passengers of the *Moresby*, which set sail from Cardiff, bound for South America, but destined for a watery grave in Dungarvan Bay. Two days before Christmas in 1895, the outbound ship had run into rough weather off Ireland's south coast and the second mate was dispatched below to fetch some plum pudding. 'Eat up boys, this is the

Launching a sail from Ballincourty harbour.

last plum pudding you will ever taste,' he shouted over the gale and in silence the crew tucked in to the far-from-festive fare. Shortly after midday both the *Moresby* and the schooner *Mary Sinclair* were spotted in trouble by the keeper at Ballinacourty Lighthouse. The schooner ran aground and the *Moresby* set anchor about half a kilometre from the lighthouse. The Ballinacourty lifeboat rowed out to see if anyone wanted to be taken off. None did, but during the night the weather deteriorated and the *Moresby* sent out distress signals. Shortly after, the anchor broke and the ship listed onto its side. Eventually the crew had no option but to jump ship and swim for it. Unfortunately, there was an ebb tide in the bay and the captain, his wife and their three-year-old daughter were swept away from the coast. By the time the lifeboat reached the scene and hauled in the exhausted sailors, out of a company of 25, only five reached shore alive.

In 1929 Ballinacourty was converted to acetylene and electrification followed in February 1964.

The lighthouse is closed to the public and there is no direct route, as it is bounded by a golf course and private property. The only way to get a good view of it is to walk along the rocky shore from the beach at Clonea or Ballinacourty Point.

The Helvick Head lifeboat patrolling the waters of Dungarvan Bay.

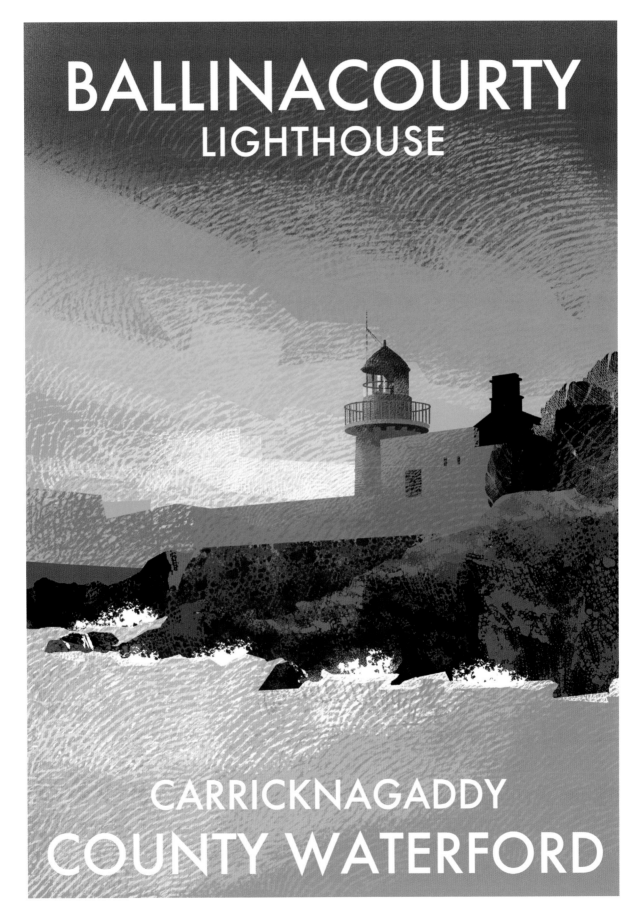

Mine Head

Location: 51° 59' 33.4" N, 7° 35' 13.5" W
Elevation: 87m
Character: Fl (4) 30s
Range: 22km

Established in June 1851, Mine Head Lighthouse rises high above the dramatic cliffs at An Sean Phobal in the Waterford Gaeltacht. The red sandstone structure is 22 metres high which, together with its lofty position, marks it as the highest light along our coast. The tower is painted white with a single black band

In the mid-nineteenth century, the merchants and shipowners of Youghal and Cork were keen for the Ballast Board to begin a lighthouse tower on Capel Island off Youghal. The chief engineer, George Halpin, begged to disagree and advised that Mine Head and Ballycotton were more suitable locations for lighthouses. Then, as now, money talks and the merchants got their way, at least for the time being. The tower on Capel Island was well under way when the business community changed their mind and agreed that perhaps the experts were right after all. Capel Island was finished only to the second storey and work began instead on Mine Head.

Kestrels at Mine Head.

Coincidentally, due to a delay caused by a damaged optic at the east Cork station, both the Ballycotton and Mine Head lighthouses were first exhibited on the same evening.

Around Mine Head Lighthouse, the wild grasslands of the clifftops attract a wide variety of seabirds much appreciated by birdwatchers and those interested in wildlife in general, while nearby a slightly older structure stands guard over the coast. The pre-Celtic Ballinamona court tomb is the only example of its kind in County Waterford. 'Cailleach Bhearra's House', as it is known locally, sits in spectacular clifftop isolation, enjoying stunning views across to the east Waterford and Wexford coastlines and perhaps into unknown worlds beyond.

The court tomb of Ballinamona.

Youghal

Location: 51° 56′ 32.3″ N, 7° 50′ 31.5″ W
Elevation: 24m
Character: Flashing, 2.5s, flash 0.5s, eclipse 2s,
Range: W: 31km; R: 24km

The name Youghal translates as 'yew woods' from the Irish *Eochaill*. The town situated on the estuary of the River Blackwater was, in medieval times, a great source of the wood, the preferred material for the longbow.

As far back as 1202, the Geraldine owners of the town built a lighthouse on the cliffs at the western side of the estuary. The original tower was 7.5 metres tall and 3 metres in diameter. The light would have been similar to that at Hook Head, being a metal brazier filled with wood, kept burning throughout the night to guide ships to harbour. To see that the light was properly maintained, they also generously endowed a nunnery called the Chapel of St Anne with the provision that the Order would be the light's guardians. The nuns fulfilled this task

Occupying the site of the former Trinity Castle, Youghal's clock tower has become the iconic image of this lovely coastal town.

until the reformation in the mid-sixteenth century when the Crown confiscated the lighthouse and the convent. The beacon was last illuminated in about 1542 and the harbour remained in darkness for over 300 years.

In 1848, due to the increased shipping using the bay, the construction of a new lighthouse was deemed necessary and the old tower was demolished. Once again, engineer George Halpin was called upon to design the lighthouse and work began immediately. The granite for the tower was, unusually, imported from Scotland rather than being quarried locally. Perhaps it had been set aside for another building. Progress was slow and it was four years before the lighthouse was ready to exhibit its light. Standing 24 metres above sea level, the light is now automated with a light flashing every two and a half seconds and reaching a distance of 30 kilometres from shore.

Below the lighthouse and the adjoining privately owned house are diving rocks, should you fancy a dip!

YOUGHAL
LIGHTHOUSE

YOUGHAL
COUNTY CORK

Ballycotton

Location:	51° 49' 33.7" N, 7° 59' 07.1" W
Elevation:	59m
Character:	Fl WR 10s
Range:	W: 39km; R: 31km

One of only two black-painted lighthouses in Ireland (the other being Slyne Head), the lighthouse at Ballycotton is accessible only by boat. Perched on the steep incline of Ballycotton Island approximately 2 kilometres from the village, the lighthouse was commissioned following the tragedy of the paddle steamship *Sirius*, which was shipwrecked here in dense fog in 1847.

The lighthouse opened four years later in 1851 and, at the time, the lighthouse keepers and their families would have lived on the island. For the children the trip to school involved rowing the distance to the mainland, if weather permitted.

This, obviously, was not ideal and, in 1896, the decision was made to move the families to the mainland. Finding accommodation was surprisingly difficult as various landlords sought to cash in on an opportunity and it was almost three years before all the families had moved ashore.

On island and remote headland lighthouses, the keepers might see no one apart from their colleagues and the crew of the relief boat during their tour of duty. Separation could be difficult both for the keepers and for their loved ones ashore. At Ballycotton, the keepers' families stood on the quay on the mainland at a certain time each day to wave to their husbands and fathers.

The Ballycotton lifeboat station was founded not long after the lighthouse, in 1858, and its most famous rescue took place in February 1936 when the lightship *Comet* stationed at Daunt Rock broke away from her moorings. The seas were so mountainous that spray was flying over the lantern of the 60-metre-high lighthouse. The RNLB *Mary Stanford* spent a staggering 49 hours at sea in a successful attempt to rescue the eight crew, having pulled alongside the floundering lightship more than a dozen times.

Perhaps because the lighthouse is tantalisingly close to the mainland, the day-to-day drama of life for the families who kept Ballycotton Lighthouse alight seems more tangible. It is therefore more plaintive to look back on the technological advances during the latter half of the last century that made this unique lifestyle come to a close.

By 1975 the light had been converted from acetylene to electricity; automation followed in March 1992. The lighthouse keepers were then withdrawn and the station was placed in the care of an attendant. The aids to navigation are also monitored via a telemetry link from Irish Lights in Dun Laoghaire.

Today, Ballycotton is one of twelve lighthouses that make up Great Lighthouses of Ireland, a new all-island tourism initiative.

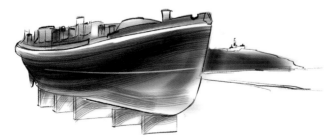

The *Mary Stanford* lifeboat, now restored by local effort, was key in many rescues when based in Ballycotton, most famously the Daunt Rock rescue in 1936.

Roches Point

Location: 51° 47' 35.2" N, 8° 15' 17.2" W
Elevation: 30m
Character: Fl WR 3s. Exhibited by day in
conditions of poor visibility
Range: W: 37km; R: 30km

In the early nineteenth century, Trinity House in London recommended the construction of a lighthouse at the entrance to Cork Harbour. Already standing 14 metres above the tide on Roches Point was Roche's Tower, which had been built by Edward Roche Esq. of Trabolgan as a banqueting room and pleasure house, with an enviable view over the entrance to the harbour and the shipping that plied those waters. A law agent was hired to negotiate the purchase of the tower and some of the adjoining land, as the owner was believed to be abroad. As it happened, Mr Roche was at that time languishing as a prisoner of war in a Neapolitan gaol and was, as a result, a little indisposed. By the spring of 1814 the board was informed that Mr Roche had at last been released and would return soon, but when he arrived almost twelve months later, his rapaciousness

got the better of him and, having demanded a king's ransom for the site, found himself the subject of an inquisition, at which the land was valued by jury. Needless to say, they didn't share his sunny assessment of the land's value, and the sum he got was a fraction of his original demand. By the time George Halpin Senior got around to assessing the ground for the lighthouse, he decided to forgo the tower and build anew further out on the point. By June 1817 the light was established, but the drama did not stop here. Just over a decade later the consensus was that the light was too small for a major port and so, in 1835, the tower was dismantled and replaced by the one which stands there today. The old tower was transported to Duncannon and erected as the Duncannon North Light, forming a rear leading light with Duncannon Fort.

On 1 April 1995, Roches Point Lighthouse was converted to automatic operation. The diaphone fog signal was replaced by an electric horn fog signal with a range of 4 nautical miles. The keepers were withdrawn and the station was placed in the care of an attendant.

The Cork Royal Yacht Club, founded in 1720 and based a few minutes upstream at Crosshaven, is the oldest yacht club in the world.

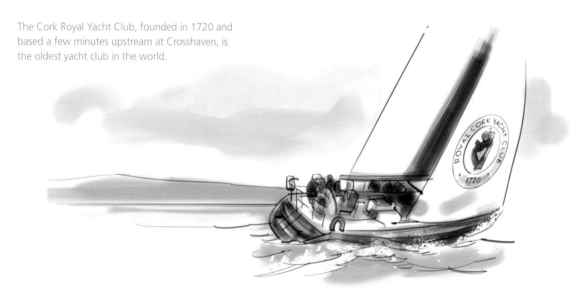

ROCHES POINT
LIGHTHOUSE

TRABOLGAN
COUNTY CORK

Spitbank

Location: 51° 50' 43.3" N, 8° 16' 27.2" W
Elevation: 10m
Character: Iso, WR 4s
Range: W: 18km; R: 13km

The Spitbank, a shallow area of mud and sand, lies opposite the town of Cobh in Cork Harbour. While it forms a natural breakwater that shelters Cobh from the worst of storm-induced swells, it presents a hazard to vessels taking the 90-degree turn to navigate the shipping channel.

In the mid-nineteenth century, overall responsibility for lighthouses in Ireland fell under the remit of the Ballast Board and in 1850 they decided that a lighthouse on the Spitbank was required. The engineer behind the unique design of this lighthouse platform was Alexander Mitchell. Blind to all intents and purposes by the age of 23, Mitchell nevertheless pursued his chosen vocation with a vigour and ambition that his sighted colleagues would envy.

Based on the humble corkscrew, Mitchell's patented 'screw-pile and mooring' technique dates as far back as 1833. It ensured that the platform would not drift. The system had been proved at Maplin Sands on the Thames estuary and Belfast Lough, and would

This statue at Cobh commemorates fifteen-year-old Annie Moore who was the first immigrant to the United States to pass through the Ellis Island facility in New York Harbour, accompanied by her brothers, Philip and Anthony.

be successfully employed in locations around Ireland, Britain and North America.

Previous attempts to construct pile-driven platforms had seen the spindly structures migrate with the sandbar, that is, if they weren't simply crushed in the process. Floating lights, traditionally used where lighthouse construction was not possible, were not ideal. The movement of the lightship altered the light's location during storms, and floating lights could break from their mooring, causing havoc for mariners.

Mitchell personally oversaw the construction, being ferried out to his lighthouse, even in rough seas (falling overboard twice), and climbing up and down ladders, crawling along planks, examining the wood, iron and rivets. Through touch he checked the quality of the ironwork, sometimes noting flaws that had escaped the labourers' or foreman's eye. One worker is recorded as exclaiming: 'Our master may say what he pleases, but I'll never believe that he can't see as well as thee or I!'

The light was exhibited for the first time in 1853 and a foghorn was added in the 1890s. Only half a kilometre from shore, but with no living accommodation on the platform, the light was managed by a principal and assistant keeper who commuted from nearby Cobh.

The light was updated and automated in the twentieth century. Now in use for over 150 years, it is one of only three remaining screw-pile lighthouses in Ireland. It was repaired following a collision in 1978, and renovated in 2013.

The Port of Cork pilot boat.

SPITBANK
LIGHTHOUSE

COBH
COUNTY CORK

Charles Fort

Location: 51° 41' 45.0" N, 8° 29' 59.0" W
Elevation: 18m
Character: Fl, 5s flash 1s, eclipse 4s
Range: W: 17km; R: 13km; G: 11km

Charles Fort is a star fort located on the rocky shoreline at the southern end of the village of Summercove overlooking Kinsale Harbour. The present light was established here only in 1929, but the site has had a lighthouse as far back the seventeenth century.

At that time, it was known as Barry Óg's or Ringcurran Castle and in 1665, King Charles II granted letters patent to Sir Robert Reading to construct six lighthouses along the Irish coast. The locations of these lighthouses were at Howth Head, the Howth bar, Hook Head, the Old Head of Kinsale,

Charles Fort and the Isle of Magee near Carlingford in County Louth. These were of the cottage style with lighted braziers on their roofs. The king got his lighthouses, the fort was rebuilt and was named in his honour. The architect of the fort was William Robertson, who also designed the Royal Hospital at Kilmainham. Star forts became popular with the arrival of gunpowder, when it was realised that the old town and city fortifications of the past were vulnerable to cannon fire. The design of the fort is normally a pentagon or hexagon with bastions at the corners of the walls. These outcroppings enable a total panoramic view of the battlefield. Because of the bastions, archers and cannon operators can hit any target on the battlefield without having to lean over the wall and expose themselves to enemy fire.

The fort was partially damaged during the Williamite War, when besieged by John Churchill, but it was repaired and continued to be used as a British military barracks until the Anglo-Irish Treaty in 1921. In 1922, during the Irish Civil War, the fort was burned by retreating anti-Treaty forces. In 1973 it was declared a National Monument and partly restored.

The lighthouse was one of the last to be converted to electricity and in 2004 it was automated and its range increased to over 16 kilometres.

The entrance to Charles Fort.

CHARLES FORT
LIGHTHOUSE

KINSALE
COUNTY CORK

Old Head of Kinsale

Location: 51° 36' 17.2" N, 8° 32' 01.1" W
Elevation: 72m
Character: Fl (2) W 10s. Exhibited by day in
            conditions of poor visibility
Range: 37km

The Old Head of Kinsale Lighthouse from the sea.

The Old Head of Kinsale Lighthouse has a long and proud history reaching back into the pre-Christian era when there are references to a lighted beacon maintained on the tip of the headland.

The first proper lighthouse, as we would recognise it, was one of six cottage-style lighthouses erected around the Irish coast in the seventeenth century by Sir Robert Reading under letters patent granted to him by Charles II. Across the road from the ruins, another lighthouse was built in 1814. It stood almost 13 metres tall with a circular accommodation block at the base. Unfortunately, this tower was frequently obscured by fog and low cloud and it was decided that a new lighthouse would be better positioned at the point of the headland.

In 1845 word was given to proceed with a new structure and within three years the new lighthouse was complete at a cost of just over £10,000, which equates to about €1.4 million today. Once the new light was established, the old tower was partially demolished so that it would not be mistaken for an operational lighthouse during daylight hours.

On the twelfth hole at the Old Head of Kinsale golf course.

In 1893 three cannons were installed as a fog signal and a signalman joined the two keepers on duty. In 1972 the light was converted to electric and the explosive fog signal was changed to a siren and then terminated altogether thirteen years later. The Old Head was finally automated in 1987, the keepers withdrawn and the lighthouse placed in the care of a part-time attendant.

Originally, the tower was plastered white with the addition of two painted red bands. This remained until the summer of 1930 when it was changed to black with two white bands.

To stand at the Old Head looking out to sea is also of course to be tragically reminded of one of the most notorious shipwrecks of the twentieth century. The RMS *Lusitania* sank just over 17 kilometres due south of the Old Head after being hit by a single torpedo fired by the German submarine U-20 on 7 May 1915. The ship listed so badly that lifeboats crashed into passengers crowded on deck and dumped their cargo into the water. The majority of the passengers never had a chance as the giant ship slipped beneath the waves in less than twenty minutes. In all, 1,198 of the 1,959 aboard perished.

Notable among the many who died was Sir Hugh Lane, the Irish art dealer and collector, best remembered for the establishment of Ireland's first gallery of modern art, which bears his name, on Dublin's Parnell Square.

Galley Head

Location: 51° 31' 47.9" N, 8° 57' 09.0" W
Elevation: 53m
Character: Fl (5) W 20s
Range: 43km

Sitting high on the southernmost point of Dundeady Island, Galley Head Lighthouse, at the time it was constructed, could claim to be the most powerful lighthouse in the world. In clear weather, the light could be seen from a distance of 30 kilometres, which was remarkable for the late nineteenth century.

Two previous attempts had been made to locate a lighthouse on the site, in 1849 and 1857, but each time funds were not forthcoming. Eventually, in 1871 Lord Bandon and a number of others wrote to the Ballast Board, pointing out the importance of a coastal light, given the number of wrecks off the headland. Figures were checked, an inspection

A view of the lighthouse through the doorway of one of the keepers' houses.

committee reported, correspondence was forwarded and in due course a lease for land was signed. Two years later, work commenced and by January 1878 the light was ready for its official launch. The light's original character was an unusual six or seven white flashes in sixteen seconds followed by a rather lengthy 44 seconds of darkness. That must have produced some anxious moments for sailors not familiar with the light's character!

Great shearwater.

The glazing on a lighthouse lantern is usually only clear where the beam needs to be directed. Consequently, at the landward side the panes are generally either replaced with copper cladding or painted out. In the case of Galley Head, all the panes to the rear are blanked off except for six panes in two faces, which have been left clear. Rumour has it that these clear panes relate to an occasion when the Sultan of Turkey was staying with Lord Carbery at nearby Castle Freke. He wanted to know what the tower on the distant headland was, and was told that it was a lighthouse, which shone out at night over the sea. The sultan thought for a moment and then suggested that it might be useful if it also illuminated the roadway and be visible from the castle. No sooner said than done! Six panes on each face were fitted with clear glass and the lighthouse stood illuminated, to the sultan's delight. While the light still shines on, Castle Freke has yet to be fully restored to its former magnificence.

Conversion to electricity was completed in mid-1969 and the assistant keeper was withdrawn and the principal keeper's wife was appointed female assistant keeper. Galley Head Lighthouse was then converted to automatic operation in 1978–9. The principal keeper retired that February and was appointed attendant from the following morning.

Today, the Landmark Trust leases the two keepers' cottages from the Commissioners of Irish Light and the restored dwellings are let as holiday accommodation.

GALLEY HEAD
LIGHTHOUSE

ARDFIELD
COUNTY CORK

Fastnet Rock

Location: 51° 23′ 21.5″ N, 9° 36′ 10.7″ W
Elevation: 49m
Character: Fl W 5s. Exhibited by day in conditions of poor visibility
Range: 50km

The 1818 Cape Clear lighthouse and signal station was the forerunner of the Fastnet Rock Lighthouse. Regularly shrouded in fog, it was abandoned in the 1840s.

The present lighthouse on Fastnet Rock is the second to be built on the island and was intended to replace the old Cape Clear light. Established in 1818, the light on Cape Clear was built on the highest point of the island's southern cliffs and was regularly enveloped in mist. This, coupled with the sinking of the packet ship *Stephen Whitney* near Crookhaven with the loss of 92 of the 110 passengers and crew on board, triggered the decision to relocate the light.

The first lighthouse to be built on the Fastnet Rock used the latest technology of cast-iron plates bolted together, with an inner lining of brick. Completed in 1854, it was not long before the shortcomings of this technique in stormy conditions became obvious. A new external casing was constructed around the tower and the cavity filled with masonry. It happened

that a nearby lighthouse on Calf Rock at the entrance to Bantry Bay had been similarly reinforced but, during a storm in 1881, the whole tower above the bracing snapped off and disappeared below the waves. Happily, no one was killed, but it certainly dispelled any complacency about the strength of the tower at Fastnet and the decision was hastily made to replace the cast-iron tower with a more resilient one hewn from granite.

The new tower took five years to build. Each granite block is dovetailed into its neighbour, bonding the structure into a virtual monolith. Every one of the 2,074 stones, weighing from 1¾ to 3 tonnes, was set by the Commissioners of Irish Lights' foreman, James Kavanagh. Despite its fortress-like construction, Fastnet was designed to bow with the gales of the Atlantic. During the most ferocious storms the top of the tower can sway as much as 3 metres from side to side. At 30 metres above low water it is the tallest lighthouse on the Irish coast.

The lighthouse is perhaps best recognised as the midpoint of one of the world's classic offshore yachting races, the Fastnet Race, a 1,126-kilometre journey from Cowes on the Isle of Wight around the rock and back to the finish at Plymouth.

The Commissioners of Irish Lights helicopter about to set down on a stormy landing platform at Fastnet.

FASTNET ROCK
LIGHTHOUSE

FASTNET ROCK
COUNTY CORK

Mizen Head

Location: 51° 26′ 59.5″ N, 9° 49′ 13.5″ W
Elevation: 55m
Character: Iso W 4s
Range: 28km

It was originally intended that there would be a lighthouse alongside the fog signal station at Mizen Head but in 1906 it was eventually decided that the signal station alone would suffice and that it should be put into the care of the keepers at Fastnet. Cloghnane Island was chosen as the site, but it first needed to be connected to the mainland. A competition was launched to design a suitable bridge. The winning entry by Noel Ridley spanned the 52-metre chasm at a height of 30 metres above sea level. An early example of reinforced concrete, it was made from the local hard stone. Even the aggregate used was crushed on site from the same rock. This original 1909 bridge lasted almost a century until 2005 when it was decided that it was unsafe. It was closed until the replacement bridge was unveiled six years later.

By 1909 the fog station had been established and the fog signal itself took the form of an explosive charge detonated at intervals.

The upside-down fog bell of the East Pier lighthouse.

A Cory's shearwater off Mizen Head.

In 1920, the Goleen and Lisagriffin brigades of the IRA raided the station in search of explosives. They made away with a half a ton of the stuff, loaded onto a horse and cart, which was then hidden around the area and later distributed throughout the brigade as required. Because no protection was offered by the government, all explosives were immediately withdrawn from the various stations around the coast and the fog signals fell silent for almost four years.

The signal was re-established on 29 February 1924 and consisted of two shots every five minutes, with a brilliant accompanying flash when sounded by night. This flash was discontinued during the Second World War as part of the blackout drill and reintroduced in 1949. The explosive type of fog signal was finally withdrawn in 1969.

A white occulting light flashing white for four seconds was established at Mizen Head in October 1959 and in October 1968 the range of the light was increased to 29 kilometres.

In 1993 Mizen Head Fog Signal Station was automated. That same year the local community in Goleen parish registered a co-operative to develop a visitor attraction at Ireland's most south-westerly point. Today, the signal station houses the Mizen Head visitor centre.

MIZEN HEAD
LIGHTHOUSE

MIZEN HEAD
COUNTY CORK

Barrack Point

Location: 51° 28' 21.3" N, 9° 23' 41.1" W
Elevation: 40m
Character: Gr Fl, 6s, 2 flashes, 0.3s flash,
1.4s eclipse
Range: R: 6km; W: 11km

Sherkin Island, or Inis Arcáin, is a small island sitting in Roaringwater Bay off Ireland's south-west coast. The island guards one side of the entrance to Baltimore Harbour. The diminutive lighthouse was built in 1885 and is maintained by the Baltimore Harbour Commissioners. On the opposite shore is the Baltimore Beacon or 'Lot's wife', as it is locally known, resembling, as it does, a pillar of salt. The two markers help mariners avoid shoals, rocks and obstacles that sound as though they come from an old book about pirates – Lousy Rock, Toe Head, Loo Rock and Ransome Point, among others.

The 12-metre south cardinal beacon at Lousy Rock next to Baltimore Harbour.

Baltimore was infamously sacked by Barbary pirates back in the seventeenth century. The attack was led by a Dutch captain, known as Murad Reis. The corsairs struck the remote village on the night of 20 June 1631. Their raid took 109 villagers, half of them children, and transported them in chains to faraway Algiers. It was the largest-ever attack by Barbary pirates on Ireland or Great Britain. Many of the prisoners were destined to live out their days as galley slaves, while others would spend long years in harems or as labourers. At most, only three of them ever saw Ireland again.

In the aftermath of the raid, the remaining settlers moved to Skibbereen, and Baltimore remained virtually deserted for generations. Today, Baltimore resonates to the sound of a different type of visitor and has a well-earned reputation as a thriving centre for sailing and as a popular venue for maritime events, such as the Wooden Boat Festival and its August Regatta.

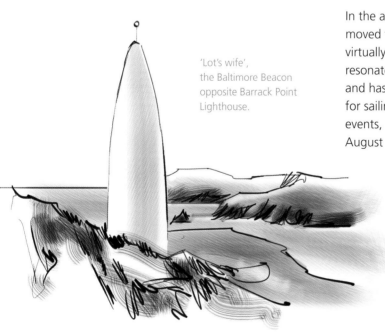

'Lot's wife', the Baltimore Beacon opposite Barrack Point Lighthouse.

BARRACK POINT
LIGHTHOUSE

SHERKIN ISLAND
COUNTY CORK

Crookhaven

Location: 51° 28' 35.6" N, 9° 42' 16.4" W
Elevation: 20m
Character: LFl WR 8s
Range: W: 24km; R: 20km

Crookhaven Lighthouse is located on the north entrance of Ireland's most south-westerly harbour and village. Today, Crookhaven is mostly visited by pleasure craft, but for centuries it was a base for fishing fleets, mercantile vessels and all manner of commercial craft.

The lighthouse dates from 1843 and is surrounded by the original dwellings formerly occupied by the keepers of Fastnet Lighthouse, Mizen Head fog station and Crookhaven Lighthouse.

The keeper of a small mainland lighthouse like this could have expected a modest wage but, to make up for any shortcomings in his pay packet, the duties

A plate of seafood, the hot summer sun and a pint to slake your thirst. West Cork at its finest!

were light. He was required to maintain the lantern from dusk to dawn, to keep all the machinery spick and span and to keep the house and tower in good order. He could also expect a generous coal allowance from the Ballast Board, but, crucially, unlike the keepers on the rock stations and even those on the remote headlands, he was not isolated from the local community.

Lighthouses are painted differently to help with their identification by sailors during the day. For example, a lighthouse such as this will typically be painted all white if its surroundings or background are dark, such as fields, woodland or mountains. The majority of coastal lighthouses in Ireland fall into this category and it helps the structure stand out from its background. All black (Slyne Head and Ballycotton), or black with white bands tend to be used where the lighthouse is silhouetted against the sky, from the sailor's perspective. Red and white stripes help the mariner identify the lighthouse if it is set against a white background, such as cliffs or rocks and, interestingly, there are no lighthouses with this colour scheme along the Irish coast.

In 1961, all the cottages bar the one adjoining the lighthouse were sold by the Commissioners of Irish Lights. By the late 1990s this too was regarded as surplus to requirements and has since become a picturesque holiday let with spectacular views across Ballydevlin Bay towards Fastnet.

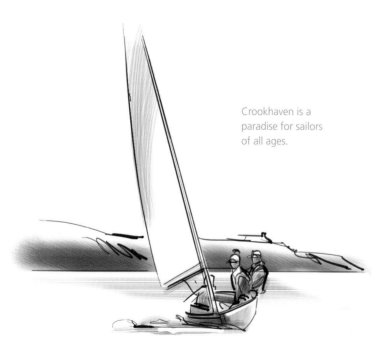

Crookhaven is a paradise for sailors of all ages.

CROOKHAVEN
LIGHTHOUSE

ROCK ISLAND, GOLEEN
COUNTY CORK

Roancarrig

Location: 51° 39′ 11.0″ N, 9° 44′ 49.4″ W
Elevation: 18m
Character: Fl WR 3s
Range: W: 20km; R: 17km

Roancarrigmore or Roancarrig serves as a harbour light, guiding shipping in Bantry Bay and lighting the eastern entrance to Berehaven. It was built on foot of a request by the coast guard service at Castletownbere in 1838. The original buildings were designed by our old friend Inspector George Halpin, and the light was first exhibited in August 1847. In September 1975 it was converted to electricity, at which time the station became unmanned.

Roancarrig is the first of a new generation of Irish Lighthouses. The Commissioners of Irish Lights designed a stainless steel tower with an array of

A Bantry Bay gig sets out.
This type of boat uses both oar and sail.

LED Lights and twelve 50W solar panels to replace the extensive masonry tower, dwellings, diesel generators, and various accoutrements of the previous station. This pillar now sits forward of the old black-and-white tower.

Shore dwellings for the keepers and their families were built at Castletownbere in the early 1900s but the station had been relieving from 1896 with the keepers living in lodgings in Castletownbere.

The island, lodgings and disused tower were recently sold and are, hopefully, enjoying a second life as a bracing retreat and holiday home.

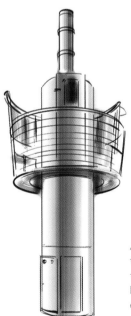

A new stainless steel tower, LED lights and twelve 50W solar panels have replaced the extensive masonry tower.

ROANCARRIG
LIGHTHOUSE

BANTRY BAY
COUNTY CORK

Sheep's Head

Location:	51° 32'35.5" N, 9° 50'55.4" W
Elevation:	83m
Character:	Fl (3) WR 15s
Range:	W: 33km; R: 28km

Sheep's Head Lighthouse, which marks the southern tip of Bantry Bay, is a relatively recent addition to the lighthouses around our coast. This remote light was installed in October 1968 to serve the development of the oil terminal at Whiddy Island.

Because of its seclusion, all the materials for construction had to be airlifted to the site by helicopter. It resembles Achillbeg Lighthouse in its design, integrating a 7-metre-high tower onto a rectangular building. Standing 83 metres above sea level, the lighthouse is looked after by a part-time keeper who lives nearby.

Sheep's Head is a special area of conservation and the peregrine falcon thrives here.

The Sheep's Head way is a very popular 175-kilometre trail that extends from the south-west mainland out into the Atlantic between Bantry Bay and Dunmanus Bay. Because of its proximity to the Gulf Stream, the climate is incredibly mild. It is an area of special protection: birds like the chough and peregrine thrive, while in the waves below, you should be able to spot seals and dolphins.

The ocean is never far away along the 175km Sheep's Head trail.

Ardnakinna

Location: 51° 37' 06.2" N, 9° 55' 05.5" W
Elevation: 62m
Character: Fl (2) WR 10s
Range: W: 32km; R: 26km

Ardnakinna Lighthouse overlooks the entrance to Berehaven sound and guards the western entrance to Castletownbere. Far below, fishing boats pass and the broad Atlantic stretches off into the distance.

Ardnakinna was established in 1850 as an unlit beacon and was left in the care of a local keeper. He remained until 1863 when the tower was capped and his services were dispensed with.

Thus it remained until pressure from mariners using Castletownbere Harbour convinced the commissioners that a light at Ardnakinna would be advantageous. Work on converting the beacon into a lighthouse commenced in 1964. As the existing beacon had been constructed as a lighthouse tower, rising to over 15 metres high at the balcony and including an intermediate floor, all that was required was a lantern to top it off. A former light-vessel lantern was sourced, modified and mounted on a concrete platform. The light was established on 23 November 1965 with a character of two white and two red flashes every ten seconds.

The ferry to Bere Island.

Bull Rock

Location: 51° 35′ 31.3″ N, 10° 18′ 04.4″ W
Elevation: 91m
Character: Fl W 15s
Range: 33km

In the spring of 1846 a request was made to the Ballast Board that lighthouses be established on Bull Rock, Galley Head and on the Foze Rocks off the Blasket Islands. Galley Head was approved but the Bull and Foze Rocks projects were postponed and ultimately the Calf Rock off the tip of Dursey Island was chosen instead as the site for the lighthouse (there are three bovine-sounding rocks in the vicinity: the Bull, the Cow and the Calf.)

The tower was completed on the Calf by autumn 1864. The lantern, optic and revolving machinery were added the following year, making the tower 37 metres high. By 1866 the lighthouse was projecting its beam out to sea. It was not to have a happy history!

Only three years later, a severe storm washed away a section of the balcony rail and a hut containing stores. The keeper ashore, thinking he saw distress

The remains of the old lighthouse on Calf Rock.

flags on the rock, launched off with six boatmen to the rescue. After battling into the mountainous swell, they arrived, only to find the keepers on the rock safe and sound. When the boat made to return to the mainland it was caught by the waves and capsized. All hands were lost.

Later, in November 1881, the lighthouse was again caught in a prolonged and ferocious storm. The gales carried away the upper section of the tower, complete with lantern, which snapped off and tumbled into the sea. By good fortune, neither the three keepers nor three workmen temporarily stationed at the lighthouse were in the upper tower at the time. All six were finally rescued from the rock – two weeks later – when conditions eased and a boat skippered by Micheal O'Shea managed to get a line to the men and bring them to safety.

With Calf Rock damaged beyond repair, a temporary light was erected on Dursey Island while consideration was given to the Bull Rock as a suitable location. In February 1882 the board finally gave the go-ahead and, having handed over the asking price of £21 to Queen Victoria for the deeds, the mammoth task of building on the rock began.

The most notable feature about Bull Rock is the natural tunnel that runs through it, giving it the air of a super-villain's lair. The lighthouse sits perched up on the rocks 91 metres above sea level. Even at this height, waves are known to crash over the lantern during particularly stormy conditions.

The station was completed in 1888 and on 1 January 1889 Bull Rock's light and fog signal were established.

The light was converted to electric power in August 1974 and in spring 1991 the lighthouse was automated and the keepers withdrawn from the station.

BULL ROCK
LIGHTHOUSE

BEARA PENINSULA
COUNTY CORK

Skelligs

Location: 51° 46′ 06.5″ N, 10° 32′ 31.1″ W
Elevation: 53m
Character: Fl (3) 15s
Range: 22km

Puffins are a common sight on the Skelligs.

Skelligs Lighthouse is one of the main sea lights off the south-west coast and is located on the outer and larger of the Skellig rocks, 13 kilometres west of Bolus Head and 20 kilometres by sea from Portmagee. This is where St Fionan established his monastery, with its collection of beehive-shaped dwellings, oratories and crosses, in the late sixth century. The beautifully crafted community of dwellings and places of worship continue to draw visitors and scholars from around the world. Since featuring in a number of the *Star Wars* sequels, the rock also attracts aficionados of the film series.

Located close to the beehive huts is a medieval chapel and two wells dedicated to Saint Michael, who, appropriately, is the patron saint of high places.

The monastery, as it is usually referred to, is positioned on the south side of the north-east peak at a height of around 167 metres above sea level.

There were originally two lights on Skellig Michael: the upper and lower. When Inishtearaght Lighthouse, 35 kilometres north of the Skellig rocks and the most westerly of the Blasket Islands, was established on 1 May 1870, the upper light of Skellig was discontinued.

During the Second World War, the Skelligs would have been a familiar sight to supply convoys plying the route from Newfoundland to Britain. In February 1944 an American flying boat, while on a reconnaissance mission to identify U-boats tailing the convoys, clipped the rock, exploded and crashed into the sea. A search by keepers and British aircraft found neither survivors nor wreckage.

By 1969, fortnightly reliefs by helicopter had taken over from the service steamer out of Castletownbere and a reinforced concrete landing pad was built on the rock near the diesel derrick at Cross Cove. The light was converted to solar power in November 2000.

Two of the beehive huts on the flank of the north-east peak.

Valentia Island

Location: 51° 56' 01.3" N, 10° 19' 16.8" W
Elevation: 16m
Character: Fl WR 2s
Range: W: 31km; R: 28km

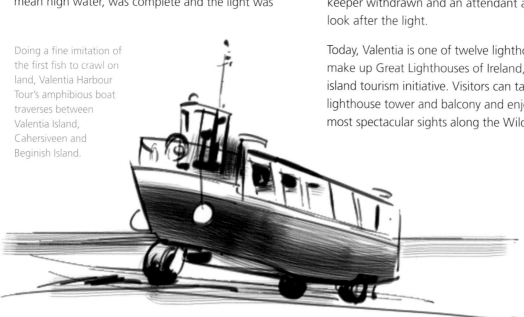

The clock tower at the harbour in Knightstown, Valentia Island.

Valentia Island's lighthouse occupies the site of what was originally Cromwell Fleetwood Fort, which is believed to have been constructed in the sixteenth century. It was one of two forts built on Valentia Island around this time. It is named not for Oliver Cromwell, notorious for the sacking of Drogheda and Kilkenny, but for Charles Fleetwood and Henry Cromwell, the Lords Deputy at the time of Old Ironside's campaign in Ireland.

A light at Cromwell Point was first suggested as far back as 1828 by the Right Hon. Maurice Fitzgerald, Knight of Kerry. After the necessary surveys, work commenced, albeit a decade later, using the original enclosure of the fort with few alterations. By February 1841 the tower, 16.5 metres above mean high water, was complete and the light was

exhibited for the first time. It could be seen 20 kilometres out to sea in clear weather. Valentia Island Lighthouse is a harbour light, intended to guide vessels from the sea and lead them through the northern entrance of the harbour past Harbour Rock.

The station was looked after by a single keeper and his family. It must have been a lonely life, wedged inside an old damp fort on the outer edge of Europe.

In November 1947 the light was automated, the keeper withdrawn and an attendant appointed to look after the light.

Today, Valentia is one of twelve lighthouses that make up Great Lighthouses of Ireland, a new all-island tourism initiative. Visitors can take a tour of the lighthouse tower and balcony and enjoy some of the most spectacular sights along the Wild Atlantic Way.

Doing a fine imitation of the first fish to crawl on land, Valentia Harbour Tour's amphibious boat traverses between Valentia Island, Cahersiveen and Beginish Island.

Inishtearaght

Location:	52° 04′ 32.5″ N, 10° 39′ 40.6″ W
Elevation:	84m
Character:	Fl (2) 20s
Range:	35km

Inishtearaght (from the Irish *An Tiaracht*, meaning 'western') is one of the Blasket Islands and the most westerly land in Europe, apart from the nearby Foze Rocks and beyond that, Iceland. The island is inhospitable – two steep pinnacles rise to 106 metres and 200 metres, joined by a saddle and a more rounded peak of 180 metres.

The Ballast Board in Ireland and Trinity House in London were in disagreement over where to site this western lighthouse. The exposed Foze Rocks were the preference of the Elder Brethern at Trinity House, but Dublin won the day and in 1864 the initial survey of the site was completed. To say that construction was a challenge would be putting it mildly. A level site had to be cleared midway up the sheer side of the island, with provision for accommodation blocks and ancillary buildings. Three keepers would have to operate here for extended periods and somehow provide for themselves in relation to food and drinking water. The Herculean task of preparing the site was accomplished by 1869 and in May the

following year, the light debuted. At the same time the upper light on the Skelligs was discontinued.

Initially, the families of the keepers also lived on the rock. The logistics of keeping toddlers away from the cliff's edge, dealing with illness, schooling and simply feeding that number of people from the scarce provisions available must have been monumental. By 1896 the station had been made relieving and the families were rehoused in Knightstown on Valentia Island.

To provide fresh milk, goats were kept on the island. They were nimble and sure-footed, more so than their keepers, one of whom fell to his death in 1913 while rounding them up for milking.

On 6 April 1988 the lighthouse was converted to automatic operation and the keepers were withdrawn from the station.

Now, aside from the puffins, petrels and a few very skinny rabbits, Inishtearaght is deserted and the lighthouse continues its lonely vigil under solar power and backup generators.

The Cathedral Rocks at Inishnabro near Inishtearaght resemble a Gothic fastness from the *Lord of the Rings* cycle.

Dingle

Location: 52° 07' 18.2" N, 10° 15' 29.8" W
Elevation: 20m
Character: Fl 3s green
Range: 12km

Dingle's most famous resident, Fungie, makes a dramatic appearance.

Dingle Lighthouse was designed by William Douglas, the engineer responsible for Fastnet, and it was built in 1885 for the cost at the time of £589, which roughly equates to €85,000 today. It guides boats seaward of Crow Rock into harbour and a welcome shelter from inclement weather. The tower stands 7 metres tall and has a range of 11 kilometres. The light is a modern acrylic Fresnel lens that gives a green flash every three seconds. The lighthouse is operated by the Dingle Harbour Commissioners.

Dingle is also the base for an active fishing fleet and the market town is a famous tourist destination, which boasts excellent restaurants and 52 pubs.

There is a nice walk from the Skellig Hotel out to the lighthouse, which follows the edge of the harbour, and takes in a picturesque cliff walk. Along the way you pass the coast guard station, which was established over 60 years earlier than the lighthouse in 1822. At the time the coast guard uniform was a navy blue denim overall with a pillbox hat. Apart from the fashion faux pas of the hat, of all the outfits to take to sea in, is there a fabric worse than denim? Unsurprisingly, the crews were known as the Bluemen.

If you're lucky, out in the harbour you might spot Dingle's most famous resident, Fungie, splashing among the waves. He has been here for almost 40 years now and unusual as it is for a lone wild dolphin to remain in the same place for such a long time, he seems to have no intention of leaving. A small cave under the cliffs at Burnham is thought to be his home.

The long and winding road to Dunquin Pier on the Dingle Peninsula.

Little Samphire Island

Location: 52° 16' 15.2" N, 9° 52' 54.3" W
Elevation: 17m
Character: Fl 5s, flash 1s, eclipse 4s,
Range: W: 26km; R and G: 20km

'Go west. young man.'
St Brendan the Navigator
points the way.

Little Samphire Island Lighthouse sits on a small rock in the spectacular surroundings of Tralee Bay. The lighthouse is a 12-metre-high, unpainted stone-built tower, enclosed by a high wall and located just south of the port of Fenit.

In the mid-1800s Fenit was an expanding centre. The only commercial port between Foynes and Cork, the harbour has traditionally served as the merchants' port for Tralee. The safety of shipping using the port needed to be assured and the Tralee and Fenit Pier and Harbour Board worked to ensure that this was the case.

In 1851, with building complete, the keepers moved into their spartan accommodation and the light was

first exhibited. While it is only a short boat ride to the mainland, inclement weather in the bay could maroon the keepers for weeks on end. With no fresh water, the keepers had to collect rainwater off the roof and ensure that no salt water had contaminated it. Having a bath was a luxury. No water was wasted and following a good scrub down, the keepers washed underwear, socks and shirts in the same water.

Visible for 29 kilometres, the light was converted to unwatched automatic operation in 1954, at which point the keepers were withdrawn.

Little Samphire Lighthouse was converted to electricity in 1976 and to solar power in October 2013.

Weather permitting, Little Samphire Island is open to the public during summer months and tours can be had of the lighthouse.

Blennerville Windmill near Tralee.

LITTLE SAMPHIRE
ISLAND LIGHTHOUSE

TRALEE BAY
COUNTY KERRY

Tarbert

Location: 52° 35' 31.4" N, 9° 21' 49.4" W
Elevation: 18m
Character: Q, 1s
Range: W: 26km; R: 19km

An old gun emplacement at Fort Shannon near Tarbert.

The name Tarbert, or in Irish *Tairbeart*, has its origins in an Old Norse term meaning 'draw-boat' or 'portage'. The town is situated in the north of County Kerry, with woodland to the south and the Shannon Estuary to the north.

The lighthouse was built on a tidal rock and was first exhibited in February 1834. It was initially operated by the Commissioners of Irish Lights and originally stood aloof from the shoreline until, in 1841, a footbridge was built, connecting it to the riverbank.

This local landmark acts as a harbour light, guiding vessels passing up and down the Shannon Estuary. The tower stands 22 metres high and contains four floors, excluding that of the lantern and gallery.

There were also originally keepers' houses built ashore of the light, but no trace of these remains.

The light shows white for 22 kilometres, with a small red sector over Bowline Rock, to the east. Originally the lantern shone a fixed light, although this was altered to a character of two seconds of light and two seconds of darkness in 1905. The landward-facing panes of the lantern housing are blacked out to stop the light spilling onto land. Mounted just below the lantern is a rotating radar antenna. The tower cannot be seen from the land, as it is in the lee of the electricity generating station, the chimneys of which dwarf the lighthouse, but it can be viewed distantly from Killimer on the opposite side of the Shannon and especially from the ro-ro ferry that plies the river crossing between the two towns.

The scale of Tarbert power station is overwhelming. Seen from this angle, the lighthouse looks tiny.

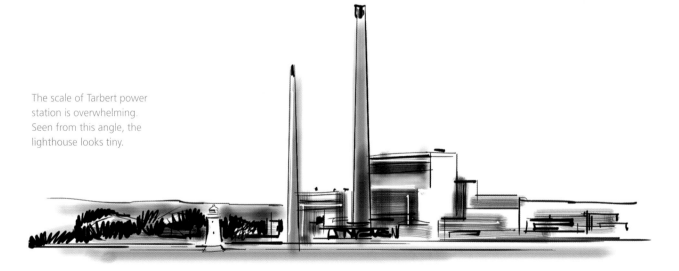

TARBERT
LIGHTHOUSE

SHANNON ESTUARY
COUNTY KERRY

Loop Head

Location: 52° 33' 40.3" N, 9° 55' 56.3" W
Elevation: 84m
Character: Fl (4) W 20s
Range: 43km

The handsomely weathered Loop Head Lighthouse is located at the tip of the Loop Head Peninsula, which is the westernmost point on the Clare coastline. The wild and rugged Atlantic coast, with spectacular views down to the Kerry coast and across to the Cliffs of Moher, provides a breathtaking backdrop to the station.

There has been a lighthouse at Loop Head since 1670. The first lighthouse was one of the six cottage-style structures built around the coast by Sir Robert Reading. It took the form of a small, cramped dwelling for the keeper and his family, with a stone staircase rising to the open roof where, in a corner, a brazier roared through the night to warn shipping of the dangerous coast. A small part of the remains can still be seen seen near the keepers' dwellings.

At the rear of the lighthouse is a gigantic EIRE sign etched into the headland. This was used to alert

passing aircrews that they were flying over neutral Ireland during the Second World War.

The area is rich in legend. The story goes that Cuchulainn was on a hunting trip in the midlands when the witch Mál caught his eye. For fear that she might enchant him, Cuchulainn took to his heels and fled west until he reached Loop Head. With a mighty leap he jumped across to the sea stack, known today as Diarmuid and Grainne's Rock, quickly followed by Mál. Back he leaped and so did she. But Mál had misjudged the distance and landed on an overhanging ledge. The rock gave way and with a mighty roar, she plummeted 70 metres to her doom in the churning waves below. Three days later, her head washed ashore, giving rise to the name Hag's Head and later her body was discovered near Quilty. To this day the bay is called Malbay. The scene of the jump became known as *Ceann Léime*, or Leap Head, which, with the passage of time, became Loop Head.

The present lighthouse, which stands 23 metres high, was built in 1854. The range of the light is 42 kilometres with a character of white flashing light four times in 20 seconds. The station was converted to electricity in 1971, and automated two decades later in 1991.

Loop Head is another of the Great Lighthouses of Ireland and managed by Irish Landmark Trust. It is possible to book holiday accommodation in the light-keeper's house.

The lover's leap. Diarmuid and Gráinne's Rock at Loop Head.

LOOP HEAD
LIGHTHOUSE

LOOP HEAD PENINSULA
COUNTY CLARE

Kilcredaun

Inactive since 2011
Location: 52° 34' 47.5" N, 9° 42' 36.0" W

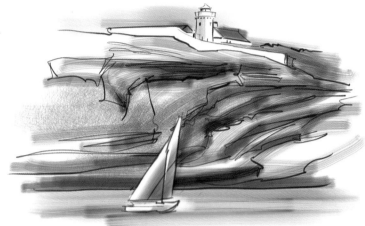

A coastal view of
Kilcredaun Lighthouse.

On 11 March 2011, after 187 years of service, Kilcredaun Lighthouse at Carrigaholt on the north of the Shannon Estuary, blinked its shimmering beam for the last time as technology overtook the past and the light was finally decommissioned.

The short, squat tower is, in fact, older than its sister at Loop Head. The original lighthouse on the head was demolished and its replacement followed Kilcredaun's debut in 1824. While Loop Head is the more famous of the two, Kilcredaun has the better views. Out on the headland you're looking across the vastness of the Atlantic, but at Carrigaholt you are looking over the estuary. Ballybunion is located about 11 kilometres across the water, while Beale Strand, the Cliffs of Dooneen and Carrigaholt Castle are all visible on a clear day.

Before the lighthouse was electrified in 1979, the lens was gas operated; the gas was manufactured on site using carbide and water. An interesting adjunct to this process was that the waste from it was used to paint most of the local houses. The sludge left over from the gas-making process resembled lime, except that its consistency was thicker and more gooey. Thinned out with water, it made an ideal whitewash.

Visible from the lighthouse is the Kilstiffin Bank, where, according to rumour, lies a submerged village. This may, in fact, refer back to the 1755 and 1761 tsunamis that inundated the south-west coast after the devastating earthquakes in Lisbon. Whatever the truth of it, local lore has it that the village rises from the sea once a year and that anyone who catches the eye of one of the residents is not long for this life!

KILCREDAUN
LIGHTHOUSE

CARRIGAHOLT
COUNTY CLARE

Scattery Island

Location: 52° 36' 20.7" N, 9° 31' 03.7" W
Elevation: 15m
Character: Gr fl (2) 8s, flash 0.5s, eclipse 1s
Range: 19km

St Senan's church on Scattery Island.

The Scattery Light was built to lead vessels to secure anchorage at Scattery Roads off the eastern shore of the island and to guide them up the River Shannon. Its construction was sanctioned by the Board of Trade in 1866. Originally, it was decided that the light should be within the boundary of the defensive battery, one of six built along the coast as fears of a French invasion mounted. To accommodate this, the light would have needed to be on rails so it could be moved in case of attack or during firing practice. Instead building began at its present site in the spring of 1868 and consisted of a simple iron framework surmounted by a lantern and an adjacent light-keeper's house. Six months later when it was destroyed in a storm, the decision was made to forgo a replacement structure and instead to build a more robust stone lighthouse tower. This was duly completed and the light first exhibited in December of 1872.

A full-time keeper ran the lighthouse until 1933, when the light was converted to acetylene and an attendant took charge of the light. This continued until 2002 when the light was fully automated.

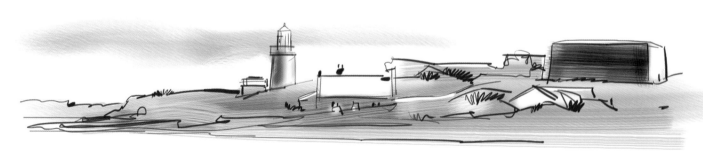

Scattery Island Lighthouse and the Napoleonic gun battery.

SCATTERY ISLAND
LIGHTHOUSE

SHANNON ESTUARY
COUNTY CLARE

Beeves Rock

Mute swans.

Location: 52° 39' 00.9" N, 9° 01' 20.4" W
Elevation: 14m
Character: FL WR 5s ,
Range: W 22km R 17km

With its lantern poking out through the roof, Beeves Rock Lighthouse on the Shannon Estuary looks like it could have come from the imagination of a sword and sorcery writer. It is accessible only by boat as there are almost no roads that go anywhere near it, which serves to add to its melancholy appeal.

Built in 1855, it was intended to shepherd shipping past the very rocks it stands on. Its unusual appearance was partly dictated by the difficulty of building on a submerged reef mid-channel. Work could proceed only at low tide and, because so little of the rock was exposed, the design was necessarily kept compact.

Its success can be measured by the fact that few vessels have sunk in this stretch of the river since its establishment. One of the more unusual wrecks to have floundered in the estuary happened in 1957 when a Dutch aircraft, carrying diamonds, crashed with its cargo. It is no surprise that this particular shipment was quickly recovered!

In the early part of the twentieth century, one of the lighthouse's keepers happened to be the maternal grandfather of former Taoiseach Enda Kenny. In 1910, James McGinley was stationed on the rock. He took time off to marry Margaret Heekin and she moved into a Commissioners of Irish Lights cottage on the mainland, near Askeaton, County Limerick. She must have spent many lonely days in the six-room house as her husband did his duty out in the estuary. From the records of the 1911 census we know she was alone at that time and signed the form 'Maggie McGinley – head of family'. Daily communication with her husband was possible only via semaphore as there were no phones or radio communication. She could see the lighthouse, and James could see her through his binoculars, but until his leave was due, this was their only form of intimacy.

The structure, with its 12-metre-high tower, was converted to unwatched in 1933 and came under the jurisdiction of the Limerick Harbour Commissioners in 1981.

The Shannon Estuary at low tide.

BEEVES ROCK
LIGHTHOUSE

SHANNON ESTUARY
COUNTY CLARE

Black Head (Clare)

Location: 53° 09' 15.2" N, 9° 15' 50.3" W
Elevation: 20m
Character: Fl WR 5s
Range: W: 20km; R: 15km

Like a homesick dalek gazing out to sea, County Clare's Black Head Lighthouse sits perched atop the otherworldly surface of the Burren coastline. *An Bhoireann*, meaning 'the great rock' or 'rocky place', forms the northern part of County Clare. Bounded by Galway Bay to the north and the Atlantic Ocean to the west, the region is an ethereal karst landscape of porous limestone that supports Arctic, Mediterranean and Alpine plants side by side, due to the unusual environment. 'Not a tree whereon to hang a man; no water in which to drown him; no soil in which to bury him' was the description of the district by one of Cromwell's generals, a man who presumably had little interest in orchids or dolmens.

After the First World War, transatlantic liners regularly called at Galway, either allowing tourists

A pearl-bordered fritillary. The rocky landscape of the Burren is home to more species of butterfly than any other region in Ireland.

to visit the city and the Aran Islands or collecting emigrants. The captains of these visiting liners were used to anchoring their vessels off Ballyvaughan, east of Black Head, and impressed on the Galway Harbour Commissioners that a light was vital to aid their mooring under the headland. Negotiations took place over the provision of a light and eventually the Harbour Commissioners agreed to cover some of the capital costs and maintenance of the light if it were installed by the Commissioners for Irish Lights. The light came into operation in 1936.

Three years later, the outbreak of the Second World War brought transatlantic liner traffic to a halt and in the post-war era it never recovered. As they collected no light dues from Black Head, the operation became a financial burden on the Galway Harbour Commissioners and they sought to divest themselves of it as soon as possible. Irish Lights were reluctant to take it over. The Galway merchants threatened to close it down. Political wheels turned in Dublin and London and eventually in 1955 it was decided that it would come back into the Irish Lights fold. Of all the participants in this wrangling, the one who came off happiest was the attendant keeper, who found that his wage under his new employer would increase by £30 per month and that he would no longer have to cycle the 9 kilometres a day to light up and extinguish the lantern!

On 18 February 2002 the gas light was changed to a solar-powered one.

The Poulnabrone Dolmen in the Burren.

BLACK HEAD
LIGHTHOUSE

THE BURREN
COUNTY CLARE

Inisheer

Location: 53° 02' 47.8" N, 9° 31' 36.8" W
Elevation: 34m
Character: Iso WR 12s
Range: W: 37km; R: 30km

Inisheer Lighthouse is a 34-metre-high sea light on the southernmost extremity of the chain of Aran Islands and guides sea traffic into the southern entrance of Galway Bay between the islands and the Cliffs of Moher on the mainland. Since 1818 there had been a light on Inishmore, near Dún Eochla, at a height of 120 metres, near to the ancient fort of the same name. Despite being placed on the highest point of the island, it was of little practical use because of frequent low cloud and mist and because as a mid-islands compromise it did not cover either the North or South Sounds adequately. As an aside, it is interesting that the fort and lighthouse get their names from the nearby village of Eochaill, which from the Irish translates as 'yew wood.' It has been a long time since a wood of any sort was seen on the Aran Islands.

By the mid-1800s the calls from the Galway Harbour Commissioners could no longer be ignored and plans were made to establish both Eeragh lighthouse on the north of the island chain and Inisheer to the south.

By late1853, the two lighthouses, constructed from the local crystalline limestone, were at second-floor level and the adjoining dwellings were near completion. Four years later, in December 1857, Inisheer Lighthouse, with a first-order fixed white light and a red sector over Finnis Rock to the east, was ready to debut and at the same time the old tower on Inishmore was discontinued.

In 1978 Inisheer was converted to unwatched electric with a standby lantern on the main lantern balcony in case of electric failure. A new LED array was installed in 2014. There is a monitoring radio link between the station and the attendant's house 2 kilometres away.

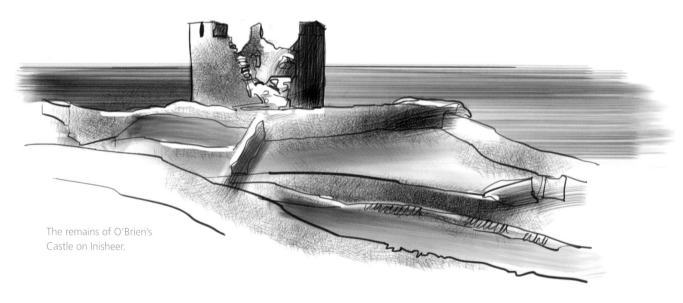

The remains of O'Brien's Castle on Inisheer.

Straw Island

A jarvey plies his trade by the harbour, by far the most entertaining way to get around the island.

Location:	53° 07' 03.9" N, 9° 37' 50.4" W
Elevation:	11m
Character:	Fl (2) W 5s
Range:	28km

Straw Island is a small, sandy island that lies at the approaches to the harbour of Cill Rónáin on Inishmore, the largest of the Aran Islands. The lighthouse on Straw Island is a small but highly important aid to navigation since, aside from fishing trawlers, the Aran Islands see a quarter of a million visitors annually travelling to their shores, mostly by water. The light was the result of a lengthy battle of letters that took place over twenty years at the tail end of the nineteenth century to have a local light built to replace the discontinued light near Eochaill on Inishmore. That light had been established in 1818 but, unfortunately, it was positioned too high, at over 122 metres above sea level, and more often than not was shrouded in cloud or mist. Its light also failed to cover the north and south approaches to Galway Bay. Inishmore was replaced in 1857 by lights on Eeragh and Inisheer.

Despite the protracted negotiations, the light was eventually established in September 1878. The tower stands just short of 11 metres high and is narrower than usual, with a diameter of just 2.4 metres. It had a principal keeper until 1913 when, for almost twenty years, an assistant keeper was instead in charge of the station. In each case, if the keeper was married, his wife acted as assistant. If the keeper was unmarried, then he was assisted by a supernumerary keeper. In 1926 the lighthouse was converted to unwatched acetylene; a decade later, all redundant rooms of the dwellings were removed, leaving just the generator house, a short corridor to the tower and two stores against the back wall.

Straw Island was converted to electricity in September 1980.

The old lighthouse and signal tower at Dún Eochla on Inishmore.

STRAW ISLAND
LIGHTHOUSE

KILLEANY BAY, INIS MÓR
COUNTY GALWAY

Eeragh

Location: 53° 08′ 54.5″ N, 9° 51′ 24.1″ W
Elevation: 35m
Character: Fl W 15s
Range: 34km

Eeragh is a sea light on the northernmost extremity of the chain of Aran Islands. The 31-metre-high tower guides traffic into the North Sound of Galway Bay.

As mentioned in the text on Inisheer, Eeragh came about as result of pressure from the Galway Harbour Commissioners to replace the 1818 Inishmore tower with lights on the north and south approaches to Galway Bay. By late 1853, George Halpin Senior recorded that the two lighthouses, constructed from the local crystalline limestone, were at second-floor level and the adjoining dwellings were nearly complete. Eeragh was first exhibited, along with Inisheer, in 1857. Originally, its day markings were white with two red bands, but in 1932 this was changed to white with two black bands.

It is only a short sea crossing to Inishmore, but the waters can be treacherous and especially in rough

A wind-powered generator at the lighthouse.

As anyone who ever watched John Ford's *Man of Aran* will remember, basking sharks are a common sight around the islands. These behemoths are gentle giants, though, and filter-feed on plankton.

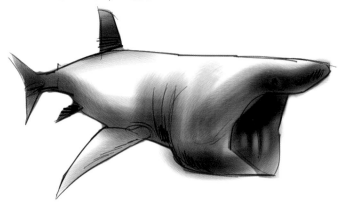

weather, the keepers could be stranded for long stretches of time. As late as 1968, a generator set was first installed to provide domestic power for the keepers. About the same time, boat reliefs were replaced by helicopter sorties originally operating from Clifden and now from Rossaveal.

John Ford's film *Man of Aran* is remembered fondly for, among other things, the sight of basking sharks feeding near the Aran Islands. Early summer is the time of year to see these migratory leviathans and the waters around Eeragh are a good place to spot them. Growing up to 8 metres long, basking sharks are the second largest fish alive today. They migrate along the world's temperate waters and – while not quite rare – are an exceptional treat to see in Irish waters. Despite being part of the shark family, they are not at all aggressive and are harmless to humans.

Automation of Eeragh took place in June 1978 and on November 2006 the light was replaced by a solar-powered light with a reduced range of 34 kilometres.

EERAGH
LIGHTHOUSE

ROCK ISLAND
COUNTY GALWAY

Mutton Island

Inactive since 1977
Location: 53° 15′ 14.0″ N, 9° 03′ 12.0″ W

The neighbouring sewage treatment plant.

Mutton Island, situated in Galway Harbour and comprising just 2 acres, was one of those very rare lighthouses where a keeper and his family lived from the start right up to automation. This was because of its proximity to the city and especially because of a sandbank, which was still in existence in the late 1800s and which was exposed at low tide and allowed access to the shore.

Weather played a big part in the keeper's life. The family depended on certain food supplies from the mainland, though they tried to be self-sufficient. The children had to be transported by boat to school on a daily basis, weather permitting.

The Scanlan family manned the lighthouse in the 1940s and 1950s. They used a series of flags to signal their requirements to the mainland. Another Galway family, the Flemings, were contracted to provide relief to Mutton Island in their *púcán* boat, (the smallest of the four types of Galway Hooker).

Mutton Island Lighthouse, one of the final landmarks of the city to be seen by emigrants leaving on the

'coffin ships' bound for the United States during the Great Famine, is currently being restored by Galway Civic Trust.

A castle and fort originally stood on the island but were demolished to make way for the lighthouse when construction began in 1815. The light was first exhibited two years later, on 25 October 1817.

The last keepers left the island in 1958 when the light became automated. The light was then turned off in December of 1977 after 160 years of service and was replaced by a candlestick-like lighthouse close to nearby Hare Island and a light buoy off Mutton Island itself.

The island is an important roosting area for a variety of birds, including oystercatchers, bar-tailed godwits, curlews, dunlins, turnstones, snipe, brent geese, swans, herons, cormorants, great-crested grebes and red-breasted mergansers. It is also, unfortunately, the site for Galway's sewage treatment plant. They are unhappy bedfellows and increased access to the lighthouse may be at risk due to safety concerns from the treatment plant.

Galway hookers.

Slyne Head

Location: 53° 23′ 59.8″ N, 10° 14′ 03.1″ W
Elevation: 35m
Character: Fl (2) W 15s
Range: 36km

Slyne Head is one of two stations on Ireland's west coast (the other being Eagle Island) where George Halpin recommended two towers rather than one. In the case of Slyne Head, there would be two revolving lights. On Eagle Island they would be stationary. This design was considered in order that the station would not be confused with Clare Island to the north or with Inishmore to the south. Once the complicated procedure of obtaining possession of the rock was done, work began in earnest.

The actual island upon which Slyne Head Lighthouse is positioned is called Illaunamid or Illaunimmul. It is the largest and most westerly of the islands forming Slyne Head. It is difficult to get to and certainly difficult to transport materials to. Consequently, the island provided all the stone for the structures and dwellings apart from some granite and sandstone.

The towers were initially painted white and were each 24 metres tall. The north revolving light gave one red and two white flashes every two minutes, while the south never had a revolving mechanism fitted and instead was a fixed first-order catoptric.

Negotiating the rocky channels around Slyne Head.

A pair of nesting shags.

In times gone by, getting relieving keepers to such a remote station was an adventure in itself. When conditions were favourable, the contracted boatman hoisted a bat or signal pole against his cottage wall as a sign to the keepers that the relief was on. He then travelled 4 kilometres across to Bunowen to alert the cart driver, who in turn proceeded to the shore dwellings at Clifden, 13 kilometres away, picked up the relief keeper, perishable foodstuffs and any other items. The horse and cart then went as far as the boat contractor's cottage, where the relief was transferred to donkeys with creels or panniers across their backs.

The donkeys then set off across the rocks and heather for a kilometre and a half to the boat slip at Slackport where the relief was finally transferred into a currach and rowed out 5 kilometres to the lighthouse through the islands and rocks which form Slyne Head. After 1969 when the helicopter was introduced, the journey took just seven minutes!

In 1895 improvements to the north tower were undertaken and a temporary framework was erected to bring its lantern above the level of the existing dome. This was deemed satisfactory and work began on replacing the 1836 lantern with a new cylindrical one, sporting diamond panes. At the same time, the southern tower was discontinued and its lantern removed so as not to obstruct the new light to the south. In 1907 it was decided to paint the two towers black as, in silhouette, their visibility to passing shipping would be increased.

The lighthouse was converted to electricity in October 1977 and was automated in 1990. The keepers were withdrawn in the spring of that year and, since then, the station has been in the care of a part-time attendant.

SLYNE HEAD
LIGHTHOUSE

ILLAUNIMMUL
COUNTY GALWAY

Clare Island

Inactive since 1965
Location: 53° 49′ 37.1″ N, 9° 58′ 59.0″ W

This dramatic lighthouse stands sentinel at the edge of the spectacular cliffs that frame the northern tip of Clare Island. Strategically positioned guarding the entrance to Clew Bay, the island is most popularly associated with its renowned daughter, the pirate queen Grace O'Malley. Granuaile, as she is also known, ruled the seas around Ireland in the sixteenth century and famously refused to bow to Queen Elizabeth I of England when they met. She considered her simply as her equal and did not recognise her as the Queen of Ireland. At the encounter, their conversation was carried out in Latin, as Ní Mháille spoke no English and Elizabeth spoke no Irish.

At the edge of the harbour on the island stands the tower house locally known as Grace O'Malley's castle and, on the island's south coast, lies St Brigid's Cistercian abbey where she is reputed to be buried.

The original lighthouse was built in 1806 by the Marquis of Sligo, at the isolated district of Ballytoughy Mór on the northern promontory of the island.

A mere seven years later the lighthouse burnt down, due to the keeper throwing the smouldering tail ends of the candlewicks into a barrel, which caught fire. A new lighthouse tower was built toward the end of 1818. Because of its height, it was often obscured by fog or low cloud and its long-term suitability was questioned. Achillbeg had been suggested as a replacement as far back as 1871, but no sanction was forthcoming to build the new light and, in 1914, Clare Island was refurbished.

By the time that automation was being considered for lighthouses around the coast, a new move to replace Clare Island was under way and a suitable site on Achillbeg was identified. On 28 September, Achillbeg Lighthouse was established and after 159 years of service, Clare Island shone no more.

Today, the listed lighthouse and adjoining buildings have been transformed into fully catered luxury accommodation, with magnificent sea views across the bay to Achill and beyond.

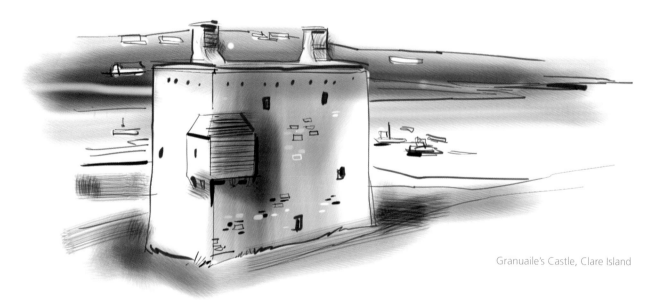

Granuaile's Castle, Clare Island

CLARE ISLAND
LIGHTHOUSE

CLEW BAY
COUNTY MAYO

Inishgort

Location: 53° 49' 35.6" N, 9° 40' 15.5" W
Elevation: 11m
Character: LFl W 10s
Range: 18km

Inishgort Lighthouse marks the entrance channel to Westport and to Rosmoney pier and pontoon in Clew Bay, County Mayo.

The lighthouse tower was originally built in 1806 and the island was one of the last places in Ireland to be connected to the electric grid.

Vessels heading to port in days past were met by a ship's pilot from the Gibbons family, who lived on nearby Inishlyre Island and who guided them through the winding channel to Westport quay.

The relatively calm inshore waters around the 365 islands of Clew Bay are fished for ray, bull huss, monkfish, dogfish and occasional tope. Large skate over 45 kilos are taken with a fair degree of regularity aboard boats anchored in the channel off the lighthouse. The fish are then tagged and released unharmed as part of a programme to help conservation and scientific research.

Nearby is Dorinish, the island that John Lennon famously purchased in the late 1960s.

The light was converted to solar power in July 2000.

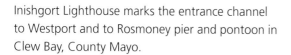

An early morning canter on the seashore.

INISHGORT
LIGHTHOUSE

CLEW BAY
COUNTY MAYO

Achillbeg

Mayo blackface sheep are a popular breed for the tough conditions, such as those on Achillbeg.

Location: 53° 51' 30.5" N, 9° 56' 50.1" W
Elevation: 56m
Character: Fl WR 5s
Range: W: 30km; R (intensified) 34km;
R 20km

In 1958, plans were afoot to refurbish Clare Island Lighthouse as the main light guiding vessels on the northerly approach to Clew Bay. It had never been entirely satisfactory as it sat high on the northern cliffs of the island and was frequently obscured by low cloud or fog. Achillbeg had been considered as a more suitable location as far back as 1871 and now a decision was made to proceed with a new lighthouse and, in the process, bring Clare Island's tenure to an end.

In 1963 a right of way was secured to the chosen site and work proceeded. In this early stage of Ireland's modernisation and before helicopter transportation had become the precision operation it is today, getting materials and transportation onto the small uninhabited island to the south of Achill itself required a little bit of graft and imagination.

Most of the materials were landed by a service tender, including a drove of donkeys to cart materials about the island. A special raft was also constructed to bring a tractor to shore. Work proceeded apace and the square concrete structure was completed with a 9-metre-high tower, or murette, surmounted by the lantern. Electricity supplied the power for the light.

The lighthouse was established on 28 September 1965, and at the same time Clare Island's 159 years of service came to an end.

The diminutive Achillbeg lighthouse on a sun-dappled afternoon.

Blacksod

Location: 54° 05' 55.4" N, 10° 03' 37.7" W
Elevation: 13m
Character: Fl (2) WR 7.5s
Range: W: 23km; R: 17km

Blacksod acts as the helicopter base
for Eagle Island and Blackrock.

Blacksod Lighthouse is situated at the southern end of the Mullet Peninsula, Erris, County Mayo.

The lighthouse was built in 1864 on land leased from, and with granite blocks supplied by, the local Reverend Palmer, who owned and administered the nearby quarry. The Reverend operated with a sharp eye for profit, unexpected in a man of the cloth. Indeed, himself, his heirs and the Commissioners would have numerous disputes over money, property access and land until Irish Lights eventually bought out the property in 1948.

The keeper's house is of an unusual design, being a two-storey, square unpainted building, with only a small conical lantern section positioned on top of it. It is set in spectacular surroundings, with the sheer cliffs of Achill Island rising to the south.

The light was first exhibited in June 1866 and it was intended that the light on Blacksod in conjunction with Blackrock, lit two years before, would make Blacksod Bay a safe anchorage. The Spanish Armada commander Martín de Bertendona, aboard his galleon *La Rata Sancta Maria Encoronada*, would certainly have appreciated it when, adrift in a storm,

he ran aground under Fahy Castle almost three centuries earlier.

During the Second World War and in the weeks approaching D-Day, the Allied meteorologists were in dispute over what the weather would be like for the week of the proposed landing. The Americans thought it would be fine, while the British thought it would be rotten. The decoded German forecast agreed with the British and Rommel left the front on a train to Berlin. The weather forecast that the Allies eventually settled on was the report supplied by Ted Sweeney at Blacksod, which convinced General Dwight D. Eisenhower to delay the D-Day invasion for 24 hours – a decision which averted a military catastrophe. It was a fateful call, and one that ensured this small lighthouse on Ireland's Atlantic coast played a part in the seismic events playing out on the European mainland.

The light was automated in 1999. Although the lighthouse is easily accessible, being beside Blacksod Pier, it is not open to the general public.

Deirbhile's Twist, a sculptural installation created as part of the Tír Sáile Sculpture Trail in north Mayo.

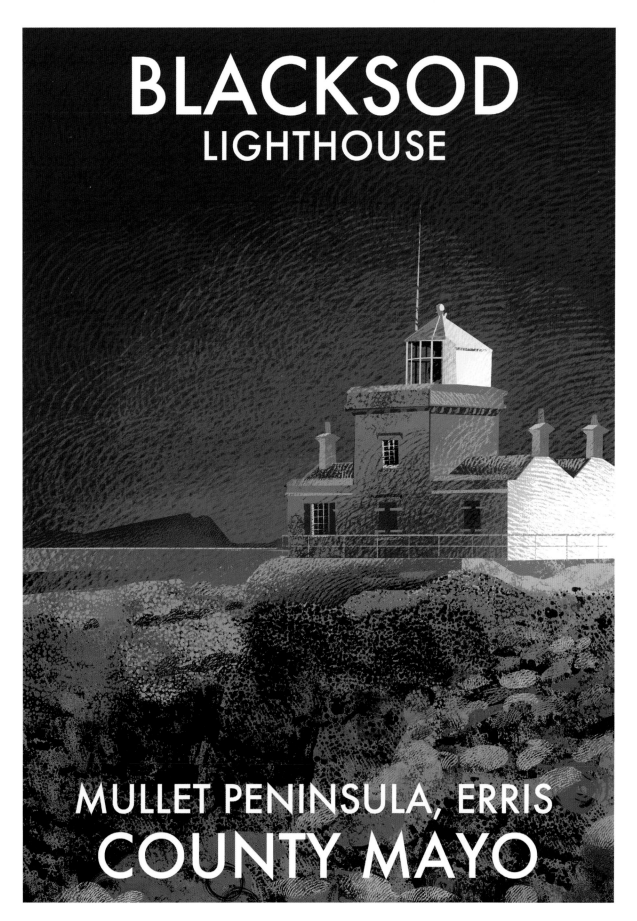

BLACKSOD
LIGHTHOUSE

MULLET PENINSULA, ERRIS
COUNTY MAYO

Blackrock (Mayo)

Location:	54° 04' 03.3" N, 10° 19' 13.8" W
Elevation:	86m
Character:	Fl WR 12s
Range:	W: 37km; R: 30km

Not to be confused with Black Rock Light in Sligo, Blackrock in County Mayo is situated about 15 kilometres west of Blacksod, out in the wild Atlantic. The idea of a lighthouse on the island was first put forward by the coast guard as far back as 1830, but it was not until almost 30 years later that the project was sanctioned by Trinity House. By 1861, the lighthouse was almost ready, but due to stormy weather neither the revolving apparatus nor the lantern could be safely landed and it was the following summer before they arrived on the island and the final phase of the operation got under way. The light debuted on 1 June 1864 and stands 86 metres above high water, with its light flashing white to sea and red to land once every 30 seconds.

On 20 August 1940 the Second World War came to this isolated outpost when the lantern panes and the roofs were shot up by a German bomber, probably a Focke-Wulf Condor, attacking the merchant ship SS *Macville*, which was sailing close to the rock. Fortunately, none of the keepers was hurt.

Being so isolated could bring other dangers to the keepers, too. In the winter of 1942/43, a prolonged winter storm trapped the keepers on the island for a record 117 days. In usual circumstances, fresh provisions would be delivered to the lighthouse every ten days, but during this unprecedented spell, the keepers had to survive on wartime rations for over 65 days before John Padden, the contract boatman, on his second attempt in three days, made the 15-kilometre trip into the teeth of the storm and managed to haul a basket of provisions onto the rock before having to retreat hurriedly across the waves. Spotting a brief lull in the weather the following February, Padden made his way back out and finally the keepers were relieved, aside that is, from the principal, Jack Scott, who stoically remained to direct operations until service was back to normal.

Eventually, in 1969, helicopters replaced the boat relief, but just five short years later the lighthouse was automated and the keepers were withdrawn.

In March 2017, while providing top cover support on a medical evacuation, the coast guard helicopter Rescue 116 tragically crashed into Blackrock. All four crew members perished in the collision.

The lighthouse sits perched near the summit of isolated Blackrock Island.

BLACKROCK
LIGHTHOUSE

MULLET PENINSULA
COUNTY MAYO

Broadhaven

Location:	54° 16' 03.9" N, 9° 53' 19.8" W
Elevation:	27m
Character:	Iso WR 4s.
Range:	W: 32km; R: 22km

First established in June 1855, Broadhaven, as the name suggest, enjoys relative calm in comparison to its neighbours, Eagle Island and Blackrock. It is positioned at the northern tip of the Mullet Peninsula and, as a harbour light, it guides vessels from seaward clear of a sunken rock on the western side of Broadhaven into a safe anchorage.

The original light was intended simply as a beacon tower, but after strong representations from local interests in Belmullet and with the general approval of the authorities, the 15-metre-tall tower was fitted with a lantern, and a dwelling and store were added. At 26 metres above high water, the light was visible for 22 kilometres, showing white to seaward and the east side of the haven and red to the west.

Broadhaven was converted to unwatched acetylene in December of 1931 and the bare stone tower was painted its present white hue. In 1946 the candlepower was increased, bringing its range to the present-day 32 kilometres. It was converted to electricity in 1971.

From Broadhaven into Blacksod Bay there stretches the remains of an ambitious canal, started in 1715 by Sir Arthur Shaen, a local landlord at Erris. His intention was to drain the marshy land, establish the new town of Belmullet and create a passage between the two bays. By the mid-eighteenth century, however, the canal was silted up and, despite work on dredging it, it remained a losing battle and maintenance ceased at the century's end. Today it is little more than a stream that dries out with the tides.

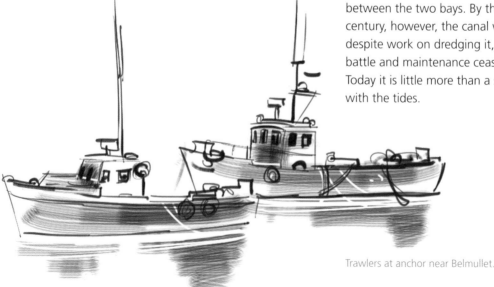

Trawlers at anchor near Belmullet.

BROADHAVEN
LIGHTHOUSE

MULLET PENINSULA
COUNTY MAYO

Eagle Island

Location:	54° 17′ 01.3″ N, 10° 05′ 33.8″ W
Elevation:	67m
Character:	Fl (3) W 20s
Range:	34km

Eagle Island is located close to the edge of the continental shelf and is constantly pounded by powerful waves from the Atlantic. According to the 1841 census, there were at that time two lighthouses and seven dwellings on the island. By the 1911 census only one dwelling house remained. Even during construction, the ferocity of the ocean was apparent when a giant wave swept the partly built west tower and all the building materials into the sea. Eventually the structures were completed and a massive storm wall was built to protect them. The east and west towers were 20 and 26 metres tall respectively and 120 metres apart, with their lanterns at the same level of 67 metres above high water. The two lights were eventually established in 1835.

It all sounds very impressive and very permanent, but the seas around this part of the western coast are relentless and a year later the western lantern was struck by rock hurled from the waves and knocked out. Quickly repaired, it was again assailed in 1850. This time the lanterns were out of commission for a

week because the repair crew could not reach the island. A decade later, in 1861, a huge wave cleared not only the island, but the eastern lantern too, smashing the windows and flooding the interior of the tower to the extent that the keepers could not open the doors and had to drill holes in them to let the water out.

Just over 30 years later, a gigantic storm at the tail end of 1894 spelled the end for families living on the island, when the dwellings at the east tower were destroyed and the storm wall damaged almost beyond repair. By 1900 all the families had moved ashore to new houses at Corclough.

Shortly after that storm, the east tower was discontinued and shortened by 6 metres so that it did not create a shadow within the arc of the new light fitted to the west tower.

The light was converted to electricity in 1968; in 2001 it was replaced by a solar-powered light with a range of 34 kilometres. The character was changed to three white flashes every fifteen seconds.

In March 1988, the lighthouse was converted to automatic operation and the keepers were withdrawn from the station.

The remains of the old East tower.

Metal Man

Location: 54° 18' 14.1" N, 8° 34' 32.7" W
Elevation: 3m
Character: Fl (3) W 6.1s
Range: 13km

The Metal Man, which is an identical twin of the Metal Man at Newtown Head in Tramore, County Waterford, was established on Perch Rock in 1821. It was originally intended for the Black Rock Beacon but when the merchants of Sligo looked for Black Rock to be converted to a lighthouse proper, the Napoleonic sailor, on their suggestion, was placed on Perch Rock. An acetylene light was established beside it in October 1908 and was converted to propane in October 1979. It became a front leading light with Oyster Island in 1932.

In March 2003 the gas-powered light was changed to solar power and its character was changed to three flashes every 6.1 seconds and synchronised with Oyster Island. Today, the light is exhibited in the hours of darkness only.

'Waiting on Shore', a sculpture at the entrance to the pier at Rosses Point, commemorates all those who were lost at sea from the area and beyond.

The statue stands about 4 metres high – bigger than life size – and is one of four casts from the original model by the Cork-born sculptor Thomas Kirk, who was also responsible for Nelson's Pillar in Dublin. The remaining two statues are unaccounted for.

An old fishing boat stranded in Rosses Point.

Oyster Island

Location:	54° 18′ 07.3″ N, 8° 34′ 16.4″ W
Elevation:	13m
Character:	Fl (3) W 6.1s
Range:	13km

Oystercatchers in the tidal mud.

Two lights were established on Oyster Island in 1837 but the one you see now dates from 1893. It became a rear leading light with the Metal Man in 1932 and was eventually converted from acetylene to propane in 1979 and then to solar power in 2003.

In 2007 at the height of the Celtic Tiger boom, the island (in part) came up for sale at a whopping €750,000. For that, you got a deserted cottage and about 35 acres. The island was famous for its oyster fishery, with beds covering an area of 70 acres. They were at the centre of a major incident in 1864 when the beds were raided by eight boatloads of men and 25,000 oysters were taken. In 1841, the population of Oyster Island was 28, mostly lighthouse employees and their families, but this figure had dropped to nineteen in 1861. The population gradually decreased and on census day in 1986, the island had one solitary inhabitant.

Life for the families of the light-keepers was tough, but on a station such as Oyster Island, probably no more so than for others of the era. Michael Hawkins, who grew up on the island in the 1930s, related how, with his father spending six weeks on Black Rock Sligo and two weeks on Oyster Island, the chores of maintaining the house – and sometimes the lights – fell to the keeper's wife and children. School was reached by rowing to the mainland but, aside from this and Sunday Mass, the family rarely left the island. They maintained a vegetable garden and some animals, while, for entertainment, card games would be played under kerosene lamps with neighbours from nearby Coney Island and Rosses Point.

Laying lobster pots.

OYSTER ISLAND
LIGHTHOUSE

ROSSES POINT
COUNTY SLIGO

Black Rock (Sligo)

Location: 54° 18' 27.6" N, 8° 37' 03.5" W
Elevation: 24m
Character: Fl WR 5s
Range: W: 19km; R: 15km

Black Rock had hosted a strategically placed beacon since the eighteenth century, helping vessels using the ports of Killala and Sligo, but a storm in 1814 washed it away. The merchants along that coast were anxious to see it re-established.

Two years later some rudimentary repair work was carried out but it was not until 1819 that a new, more solid, unlit beacon, 15.5 metres high, was built.

It was proposed that a 'metal man' would be erected on top of the beacon, identical to the one at Newtown Head in Tramore, but the local shipowners were less than enamoured with that idea and pushed for the existing beacon to be converted to a proper lighthouse, while the Metal Man should be positioned on Perch Rock off Oyster Island in Sligo Harbour.

'Panniers' were added to Black Rock Lighthouse in 1863 to provide extra accommodation. They were removed in the early 1970s.

The Metal Man got his perch, but the lighthouse had to wait another twelve years. The solid beacon was used as the base of the new 25-metre tower, hence the outside spiral staircase to the entrance door well above the high-water mark. The light was established on 1 June 1835 and, in 1863, two panniers, or additional rooms, were added to the outside of the structure about midway up. These were necessary extra stores given that half of the tower was a solid mass. In the 1930s, the tower's colour was changed from all white to white with a black band in the centre. Originally oil-fired, the lighthouse was converted to acetylene in 1934 and to electricity in September 1965. The panniers were removed in the 1970s.

Surfing in nearby Strandhill.

St John's Point (Donegal)

Location: 54° 34' 09.7" N, 8° 27' 39.4" W
Elevation: 30m
Character: Fl W 6s
Range: 26km

There are two St John's Point lighthouses along our shores. One is in County Down and the other is here at the far end of St John's Point, Dunkineely, County Donegal on one of the longest peninsulas in Ireland.

The lighthouse is a harbour light designed to guide vessels from Donegal Bay and is also used to mark the north side of the bay leading to Killybegs Harbour from the entrance up to Rotten Island.

The lighthouse dates back to the early 1800s. The Ballast Board received a petition on 24 February 1825, signed by merchants and traders from what was then and still is the largest fishing port in County Donegal: Killybegs. They urgently sought a light to

A chough, or sea crow.

be established at St John's Point to serve the port, but the wheels of progress move slowly and it was another four years before the sanction to commence was approved.

George Halpin Senior was tasked with designing and overseeing the lighthouse's construction. The tower eventually stood 30 metres above high water and had a first-order catoptric fixed light with clear weather visibility at 26 kilometres. The light was first exhibited before the final completion of the lighthouse on 4 November 1831 and the actual build was not completed until the tail end of 1833.

St John's Point moved to an automatic unwatched operation in November 1932 and was converted from acetylene to electricity with a diesel generator on standby in September 1962.

Another of the Great Lighthouses of Ireland initiative, you can now stay in one of the two light-keepers' cottages managed by Irish Landmark Trust.

With the abundance of marine life, St John's Point is a popular spot with scuba divers.

Rotten Island

Location: 54° 36' 52.7" N, 8° 26' 26.1" W
Elevation: 20m
Character: Fl WR 4s
Range: W: 28km; R: 20km

Not the setting from a Stephen King horror novel, Rotten Island is instead a harbour light that illuminates the passage from St John's Point to the inner channel and past the rocks to anchorage within Killybegs Harbour.

Requested by the commander of the coast guard, who wrote to the Ballast Board in 1832, it is once again the work of George Halpin Senior. The light was established in 1838 and the 14-metre-high, cut-granite tower painted white. Tragically, three workers drowned during construction when their boat capsized.

The barnacle goose is a frequent visitor to the south Donegal shores from their breeding grounds in Greenland.

The lighthouse is a familiar sight to the fleets of fishing trawlers that ply the waters off our western coast and must be a welcome sight for those returning to shore after a long period out on the fishing banks.

The station became unwatched on 7 January 1959 and was converted to dissolved acetylene. The new fuel, however, was considered by many of the mariners using the harbour to give an inadequate light and it was quickly converted to electricity with an increase in power to 13,000 candelas in the white sector and 2,600 in the red. The white sector has a range of 28 kilometres, while the red's range is 20 kilometres.

The Bundoran lifeboat in action.

ROTTEN ISLAND
LIGHTHOUSE

KILLYBEGS
COUNTY DONEGAL

Rathlin O'Birne

Location: 54° 39′ 49.0″ N, 8° 49′ 57.1″ W
Elevation: 35m
Character: Fl WR 15s.
Range: W: 22km; R: 18km

Rathlin O'Birne Lighthouse sits perched on the western edge of a small, uninhabited, low-lying island, indented on all sides by channels and bounded by cliffs. The island also has a sea arch in its northern part and is the westernmost point of County Donegal. It is located at the tip of the sea entrance to the Slieve League cliffs and 1.5 kilometres west of Malin Beg Head and should not be confused with Rathlin Island off the coast of County Antrim.

The island's position and its lack of cover leave it very exposed to western gales and the road from the landing stage to the lighthouse is protected by two unusually tall cut-stone walls, 2 metres high and set 3 metres apart, designed to protect the lighthouse keepers against the worst of the Atlantic winds on their journey from the beach.

The lighthouse came about as a result of a submission from the shipowners of Sligo who emphasised the need for a light on Raughley Bourne, as it was then known, on the western Donegal coast. The Ballast

Board were in favour and plans were prepared. It took a decade, however, before anything significant happened and it was 1856 before the light was eventually established. Until 1912, the keepers lived on the island with their families – a situation made possible by the existence of a freshwater spring near the dwellings – in what must have been an uncomfortable and claustrophobic existence, separated from the mainland by 2 kilometres of a sound with dangerous currents running through it. By Christmas of that year, much to their joy, the families had moved into new dwellings in nearby Glencolmcille.

It is not clear how the island came by its name, but it appears to have been associated with a clan by the name of Birn. No official records exist to confirm whether they were local or came from elsewhere in Ireland. We do know, however, that Saint Patrick's coppersmith and the first Bishop of Elfin, Saint Asicus, came to Rathlin O'Birne Island and lived as a hermit there for seven years until some of his flock rowed out and brought him back to the mainland.

In 1974 a radioisotope thermoelectric generator was installed, making it home to Ireland's first nuclear-powered lighthouse. However, by 1987 the nuclear battery had become worn down and the lighthouse was converted to wind power. This was replaced by solar energy in 1991, and that remains its fuel source to this day.

The high stone walls from the landing stage to Rathlin O'Birne Lighthouse sheltered the keepers from the worst of Atlantic gales.

RATHLIN O'BIRNE
LIGHTHOUSE

RATHLIN O'BIRNE ISLAND
COUNTY DONEGAL

Ballagh Rocks

Location: 54° 59' 57.8" N, 8° 28' 50.3" W
Elevation: 13m
Character: Fl W 2.5s
Range: 9km

Running between Burtonport on the mainland and Arranmore is a stretch of water known as the Arranmore Roads. At its northern end is Ballagh Rocks, the largest of a group known as the Blackrocks. It is a very exposed corner of the country and, owing to high seas experienced on this wild coast, it presents a danger to shipping.

As far back as 1867, it had been recommended to construct an unlit beacon on the rocks and, when the 9-metre-tall conical tower was eventually erected eight years later, it was hailed as a great success by seafarers. In the mid-1920s a black band was added to its waist and after that it was decided to leave well enough alone.

It was almost 60 years before any substantial improvements were considered, when, in 1979, it was decided to light it and convert it to a 'west cardinal' beacon. Using propane gas, however, it proved impossible to provide the nine quick flashes

every fifteen seconds as required and supplying the beacon with acetylene involved logistical difficulties. In the end, it was decided to re-character the beacon as a lighthouse using easily available propane and a lantern was placed on top of the beacon and a store constructed.

During the building phase, one of the construction helicopters, carrying an under-slung container of concrete, was forced to ditch into the sea between Arland's Point and Ballagh Rocks. The pilot managed to exit the sinking craft and was picked up by the attending boat, which, luckily, happened to be in the vicinity.

The new light was exhibited on 21 May 1982 with a one-second white flash every two and a half seconds. Ballagh Rocks was converted to electricity-using batteries in May 1983.

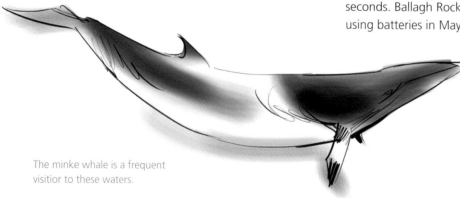

The minke whale is a frequent visitior to these waters.

BALLAGH ROCKS
LIGHTHOUSE

ARRANMORE ROADS
COUNTY DONEGAL

Arranmore

A white-tailed sea eagle.

Location:	55° 00' 54.2" N, 8° 33' 40.0" W
Elevation:	71m
Character:	Fl (2) W 20s. Auxiliary Light Fl R 3s over Stag Rocks
Range:	50km

Arranmore Lighthouse can be found in the north-west corner of Arranmore Island facing out into the wide Atlantic ocean. There has been a lighthouse here since 1798, but it was decommissioned in 1832 with the opening of Tory Island Lighthouse. It was opened again in 1859, thanks to a deluge of requests from mariners, and featured a new 23-metre-tall tower designed by the redoubtable Mr George Halpin, who made good use of the masonry from the old structure in the process. It was fitted with a second-order dioptric removed from Rathlin O'Birne the previous year.

Its proximity to the Atlantic Ocean mercantile corridor meant that the lighthouse was used as a Second World War observation post, keeping a look out for U-boats. Arranmore (*Árainn Mhór*) is in the Gaeltacht, or Irish-speaking, area of Donegal and is less than 5 kilometres from the Donegal mainland

coast. Its combination of hills, rocky mountainsides and small lakes make it a popular holiday destination, especially for those who like walking.

Mains electricity came to the island in the late 1960s and a mains supply was completed to the lighthouse in 1970. Conversion of the lighthouse to automatic operation took place in 1976 and the keepers were withdrawn on 1 August 1976.

In the course of my research for this station I spotted a heading: 'Arranmore Light yarn,' and I thought I had come across some juicy lighthouse gossip from days gone by. Instead I was introduced to the delights of a fine-weight tweed yarn that is 80 per cent merino wool, 10 per cent cashmere and 10 per cent silk. If knitting is your thing, you should look it up!

The Arranmore lifeboat.

ARRANMORE
LIGHTHOUSE

OILEÁN ÁRAINN MHÓIR
COUNTY DONEGAL

Tory Island

Location:	55° 16′ 21.4″ N, 8° 14′ 57.8″ W
Elevation:	40m
Character:	Fl (4) W 30s, night-time only
Range:	34km

Out beyond Donegal's Bloody Foreland, almost 15 kilometres adrift from shore in the wild Atlantic Ocean, sits Tory Island or *Toraigh* or *Oileán Thúr Rí*. This ancient ridge-backed settlement bears the brunt of the ferocious winds of the North Atlantic, winds which have eroded the cliffs of the island into ranks of gigantic 'tors' or pillars and from these, the island gets its name, Tory, or locally, Torry. It is a part of the Donegal Gaeltacht and Ulster Irish is the main language spoken on the island.

Because the prevailing winds run parallel to the coast, the spores that spread the potato blight during the Great Famine never quite took hold on the island.

The Tau Cross on Tory Island. The tau shape is one of the oldest representations of a cross because the crosses used by Romans for crucifixion were T-shaped rather than the more familiar shape represented today.

Consequently it survived into the twentieth century with a healthy population, but the intervening years, modernisation and the island's isolation have not tempted the young to remain and, at last count, the number of residents had fallen below 150.

The light was established on 1 August 1832, once again at the behest of the Sligo merchants and shipowners, an obviously vocal and persuasive group of businessmen. George Halpin got to work designing the lighthouse and under his supervision the 27-metre-high tower was ready to debut in less than four years. From the start, the lighthouse played a big part in the community of Tory, providing work in its construction and then in provisioning and at times in staffing the station.

The light, with its all-seeing single eye, must surely have reminded some islanders of Tory's ancient myth of Balor of the Evil Eye. This King of the Fomorians, a piratical race similar to the Greek Titans, terrorised the Irish coast in prehistoric times and is forever associated with Tor Mór, the highest point on the island where he is said to have imprisoned his daughter Ethlinn in an attempt to avoid a druid's prophecy that he would be killed by his own grandson. As is the way of these epics, of course, the prophecy was fulfilled in an unexpected manner. I won't spoil the story for you, but you can be sure that Balor meets a grisly end.

Originally, the light was fuelled by oil. This was replaced by gas, which was made at the station, and then vaporised paraffin. Electricity came in 1972.

The tower had traditionally been painted all black, but in 1956 the present white band was added at the tower's midriff. In March 1990 the lighthouse was converted to automatic operation and the keepers were withdrawn from the station.

TORY ISLAND
LIGHTHOUSE

OILEÁN THORAÍ
COUNTY DONEGAL

Fanad Head

Location: 55° 16' 34.5" N, 7° 37' 55.3" W
Elevation: 39m
Character: Fl (5) WR 20s
Range: W: 34km; R: 26km

Standing between the glacial fjord of Lough Swilly and sandy Mulroy Bay, Fanad Head Lighthouse has one of the most spectacular settings of any lighthouse on Ireland's shores. The lighthouse is classified as a sea light, rather than a harbour light, although it does mark the entrance into Lough Swilly, which forms a natural, sheltered harbour. Its location within the Donegal Gaeltacht, on the eastern shore of the Fanad Peninsula, is truly breathtaking, making it one of the highlights of the Wild Atlantic Way.

Following a tragedy 200 years ago, a lighthouse at Fanad was deemed essential to seafarers. In December 1811, the frigate *Saldana*, seeking shelter from a storm, headed towards Fanad as it frantically fought the raging wind and waves. Sadly, it never reached shore and the ship was wrecked off the peninsula – its only survivor was the ship's parrot, recognisable as such from the inscribed silver collar it wore.

In 1814 sanction was given to proceed on building a lighthouse at Fannet Point, as it was called, and George Halpin was given the task of designing

the structure. The light was first exhibited three years later in March 1817 and its fixed non-flashing catoptric light showed red to sea and white to the lough. As far back as 1871, the Duke of Abercorn was pressing the Ballast Board to improve the light at Fanad, but it was not until 1909 that a new revolving third-order lens was fitted. This remained in place until the station was converted to unwatched electric in 1975 and the apparatus was replaced, giving group flashing five white and red every twenty seconds with the nominal range of the auxiliary light increased to 28 kilometres.

In 1969 helicopters were introduced to provide the reliefs at rock stations from Fastnet in the south-west to Inishtrahull on the north coast. Fanad Head was chosen as the land base for Tory Island and Inishtrahull.

Fanad is one of the twelve lighthouses which make up Great Lighthouses of Ireland, an all-island tourism initiative giving visitors the opportunity to visit or stay in a lighthouse.

FANAD HEAD
LIGHTHOUSE

EARA THÍRE NA BINNE, BAILE LÁIR
COUNTY DONEGAL

Dunree

A British First World War
coastal defence gun at Fort Dunree.

Location:	55° 11' 53.3" N, 7° 33' 15.0" W
Elevation:	46m
Character:	Fl (2) WR 5s
Range:	W: 22km; R: 17km

Dunree Lighthouse on the Inishowen Peninsula is built 46 metres above the high-water sea level and commands a spectacular position overlooking over Lough Swilly and out to the wild Atlantic. It was built in 1876 after the Duke of Abercorn requested better lighting for the lough and suggested converting the two forts at Macamish and Dunree. These two Martello towers had been built by the Royal Navy during the Napoleonic Wars and were of strategic importance in guarding the entrance to Lough Swilly. The threat of invasion was not deemed over and the government was reluctant to dispose of the towers. Following a survey of numerous potential sites, a position on higher ground to the north was settled on. It had the advantage that, at this height,

it needed to be no higher than a single storey and so the lighthouse was designed with the lantern attached at ground level to the front of the dwelling.

The character of the light is two flashes of white/red every five seconds. Its range is 22 kilometres (white) and 17 kilometres (red). In 1927 the light was converted to unwatched acetylene, which meant that the then keeper, John Murphy, no longer had to keep a night watch. The light was converted to electricity in 1969.

In 2015 a new automated light was installed seaward of the old lighthouse, with an elevation of 49 metres. Its range and arc remain unchanged.

The impressive Fort Dunree.

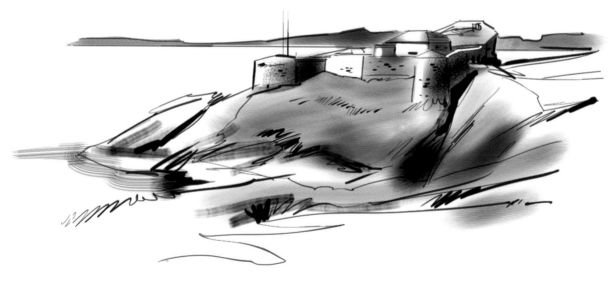

DUNREE
LIGHTHOUSE

INISHOWEN PENINSULA
COUNTY DONEGAL

Moville

The sixth-century Skull House near Moville. Often associated with St Finian, it may once have served as an oratory.

Location:	55° 11′ 00.0″ N, 7° 02′ 07.2″ W
Elevation:	11m
Character:	Fl W 2.5s
Range:	7.5km

Built in 1882, Moville is the largest of a series of pile lighthouses built at the end of the nineteenth century. The lighthouse is one of just three of its kind remaining in Ireland, the others being at Dundalk and Cobh (Spitbank).

The engineer behind the unique design of this lighthouse platform was Alexander Mitchell, who by age 23 was, to all intents and purposes, blind. He nevertheless pursued his chosen vocation with a vigour and ambition that belied his disability.

Based on the humble corkscrew, Mitchell's patented 'screw-pile and mooring' dates as far back as 1833. It ensured that the platform would not drift. The system had been proved at Maplin Sands and Belfast Lough and would be successfully employed in locations around Ireland, Britain and North America.

Previous attempts at pile-driven platforms had seen the spindly constructions migrate with the sandbar, if they were not simply crushed in the process.

Floating lights, traditionally used where lighthouse construction was not possible, were not ideal. The movement of the lightship altered the light's location during storms, and floating lights could break from their mooring, causing havoc for mariners.

In 2009 restoration work was carried out by Derry Port and Harbour Commissioners, and involved replacing the handrail around the outside and the door of the housing on top, as well as refurbishing the housing and painting the cast-iron structure. The original fuel used in the light was paraffin, then gas and most recently solar power. The keepers, who lived in Moville, would row out to the lantern at dusk, light the lamp and remain overnight in the watch room on the deck in case the light failed.

Moville Lighthouse sits a half kilometre offshore from the town and is 13 metres high. It flashes once every two and a half seconds with a range of 6.5 kilometres with a red sector covering Moville Bank inshore. It is one of a number of lighthouses on the lough and responsibility for its operation and maintenance rests with the Harbour Board in Derry.

Down by Moville harbour.

MOVILLE
LIGHTHOUSE

INISHOWEN PENINSULA
COUNTY DONEGAL

Stroove

Location: 55° 13' 34.0" N, 6° 55' 44.9" W
Elevation: 29m
Character: Fl (2) WRG 10s
Range: W: 33km; R: 26km; G: 30km

At Stroove beach.

With the increase in maritime traffic coming to Derry port in the early 1800s, the Chamber of Commerce and the Derry Ballast Board were anxious to have a light established to assist vessels negotiating the Tuns Bank, a spit of sand north-east of Magilligan Point on the Derry shore and a clear danger to shipping. The preferred position was on the Donegal shore at the entrance to Lough Foyle and George Halpin was set the task of surveying the approaches and making recommendations. His advice was that two lights be established and, with sanction approved, work began on the two towers and associated dwellings. When built, the cut-stone lighthouses, bearing east and west, stood 50 metres apart with each tower 15 metres high. They were both painted white and stood 20 metres above high water.

However, the lights, both established in December 1837, had been constructed without any distinctive character and were easily confused with each other. Various remedies were tried, such as introducing lights at midway and using a red sector on the west light, but the fact that the two towers were of the same height doomed any short-term fix. The amount of correspondence between all the interested parties could have built a third tower and during over 100 years of trial and mostly error, there was little illumination when it came to providing a long-term solution. The issue was eventually forced with the arrival of electricity in the 1950s when it was decided to replace the rear acetylene light with an electric light in a catadioptric lens with a red sector over the Tuns Bank. At the same time, the front light would be abandoned and its lantern removed. The station was automated in September 1979 and in May 2007 the fog signal was permanently disestablished. The light continues to be exhibited in conditions of poor visibility during daylight, alongside the usual hours of darkness.

Port a Doris is a small, natural doorway in the rock that leads to a hidden pebble beach near the lighthouse.

STROOVE
LIGHTHOUSE

GREENCASTLE, INISHOWEN
COUNTY DONEGAL

Inishtrahull

Location:	55° 25′ 51.8″ N, 7° 14′ 37.7″ W
Elevation:	59m
Character:	Fl (3) W 15s. Shown by day in poor visibility
Range:	35km

Inishtrahull or '*Inis Trá Thuathail*' as used by speakers of Donegal Irish, roughly means 'Island with the beach on the opposite side'. Usually the preferred landing place on an island faces the mainland, but on Inishtrahull, the opposite is the case.

The island about 10 kilometres north of Malin Head, hosts the most northerly of Ireland's lighthouses and, together with Tory Island, forms the two main landfall lights for shipping from the Atlantic rounding the north coast of Ireland, alongside navigation to local shipping. The island had a resident community until 1929 and the lighthouse

The island had been uninhabited since 1928. Scattered on the island are ruined cottages and lazy beds, while beside the old schoolhouse there is an inscribed cross, possibly a Mass Rock, and at least one grave.

was manned until 1987. Today it is uninhabited and has been designated a protected area on account of its wildlife.

On the eastern side of the island are the ruins of the old lighthouse, the first to be built to the designs of George Halpin by the Ballast Board as far back as 1813. Commissioned largely at the behest of the Royal Navy who used Lough Foyle as their North Atlantic base, the light was a revolving unit until the 1860s when it was replaced by a first-order dioptric and a new lantern. Its character was one flash every two minutes and this was changed to one every minute in 1873, only to discover that this was identical to Skerryvore off the Scottish coast, and so it was hurriedly changed back.

In 1900, after lengthy discussions, a fog signal was built on the west end of Inishtrahull, which meant that the keepers had to go from one end of the island to the other during foggy weather. In 1952, when the Commissioners of Irish Lights were looking at replacing the fog-signalling machinery and updating the lighthouse, they decided to build anew on the island's western end. The new reinforced concrete tower had the fog signal built above the light. The light first exhibited in October 1958. The light was automated in March 1987. In 2000, Inishtrahull was converted to solar power and its range reduced to 35 kilometres.

INISHTRAHULL
LIGHTHOUSE

INISHTRAHULL ISLAND
COUNTY DONEGAL

Rathlin West

Location: 55° 18' 03.1" N, 6° 16' 48.9" W
Elevation: 62m
Character: Fl R 5s
Range: 41km

Off the north Antrim coast, Rathlin West at Crockantirrive is one of three lighthouses on the island. Settling on this location for the lighthouse caused much discussion between Trinity House in London and the newly established Commissioners of Irish Lights. An alternative position at Bull Point was favoured by some and it was even suggested that the fog station be at one location and the lighthouse at the other. Luckily, sense prevailed, and the cliff-side setting here at Crockantirrive was chosen. The designer C.W. Scott was determined to avoid the errors of previous lighthouses that were placed at too high an elevation and so occasionally obscured by fog or low cloud. He decided to invert the light and built it into the cliff below the dwellings and storerooms. Construction took place between 1912 and 1917. The huge bank built at 45 degrees to the cliff consumed tonnes of concrete and, to

Rathlin Island is famous for its puffins.

facilitate the transporting of materials for the new lighthouse, a new pier and an inclined railway had to be built at Corraghy.

The 'upside-down' lighthouse was first established in March 1919 and later converted from a manned paraffin light to an unwatched electric. It is now monitored from Rathlin East Lighthouse. On 30 November 1983 it was automated.

Rathlin West is one of the Great Lighthouses of Ireland tourism initiative and the lighthouse can be visited.

The spectacular cliffs that support the 'upside-down' lighthouse.

RATHLIN WEST
LIGHTHOUSE

RATHLIN ISLAND
COUNTY ANTRIM

Rathlin East

Location: 55° 18′ 06.7″ N, 6° 10′ 18.8″ W
Elevation: 74m
Character: Fl (4) W 20s. Exhibited throughout 24 hours
Range: 48km

Rathlin East Lighthouse is the location from which the world's first commercial wireless telegraphy link was established by employees of Guglielmo Marconi, transmitting to Kenmara House in Ballycastle, County Antrim on 6 July 1898. Rathlin is the only inhabited offshore island of Northern Ireland, with a population of approximately 150 people, down from more than 1,000 in the late nineteenth century. It is the most northerly inhabited island off the coast of Ireland.

There are three lighthouses on the island: East, West and Rue Point. The eastern light was established in 1856. Originally, the tower was unpainted. Then it was painted overall white with a red band below the balcony and finally, in 1934, this band was changed to black. In 1866, a fog signal was established at the light, which consisted of an 18-pounder gun that was fired every twenty minutes during fog conditions. Over the years, the frequency of the detonation was increased to fifteen minutes, then eight minutes. After the First World War, the fog gun was replaced by an explosive fog signal, consisting of a double tonite explosion every five minutes. By the mid-1960s, the fog signal had escalated to an explosive, accompanied by a brilliant flash of light when sounding during hours of darkness. The whole shebang was understandably discontinued in 1972 for security reasons along with other similar fog signals around the coast. The lower fixed light was discontinued in 1894 and at the same time the tower light was intensified. The lighthouse operated with a vaporised paraffin burner giving four flashes every twenty seconds until conversion to electricity in 1981. Fourteen years later, in 1995, the station was automated and the keepers withdrawn.

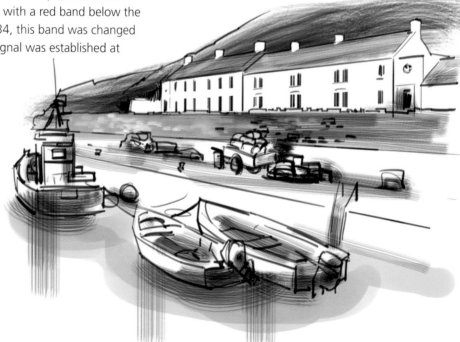

Rathlin Island harbour.

Rue Point

Location: 55° 15' 32.0" N, 6° 11' 28.4" W
Elevation: 16m
Character: Fl (2) W 5s
Range: 26km

Guillemots on Rathlin Island.

Situated at the southern tip of Rathlin, only 2 kilometres from Fair Head, an unwatched light at Rue Point was recommended as far back as July 1914. The following year, a temporary white double flashing light was erected for the Admiralty, without issuing a notice to mariners, and Rue Point came into operation. Because of the high cost of operating the light, a more permanent structure was proposed, but with a world war in progress, the Board of Trade was unwilling to consider such expenditure. An acetylene fog gun had also been recommended and this went into operation in 1917. Later that year, a severe storm destroyed the temporary light and its replacement was transferred to the fog-gun trestle.

It was not until 1920–21 that the six-sided tower we see today was eventually built, incorporating the fog gun on its roof.

In its early days, two keepers had been assigned to the station, living in a nearby wooden hut when on duty. After the fog gun once more broke down, plans were made to replace it with a more reliable model and withdraw the keepers. It was another three years before this was achieved. The fog gun was overhauled and it then replaced the old fog bell at Barr Point by the entrance to Larne Lough.

In 1965, Rue Point was converted from acetylene to electricity and is now monitored from Rathlin East.

The spectacular view of the Causeway Coast from Rue Point.

The Maidens

Location: 54° 55' 44.9" N, 5° 43' 40.1" W
Elevation: 29m
Character: Fl (3) W 15s 24h
Range: 43km

Manx shearwaters glide over the tide.

The Maidens (or Hulin Rocks) comprise two islets and several reefs off the County Antrim coast. Lighthouses were originally built on both rocks, the East Tower on the Southern Rock, which lies about 9 kilometres from the coast at Ballygalley and 20 kilometres from Larne, and the West Tower on the Northern Rock, which is less than a kilometre further out. It is hard to conceive of now but from the start, the keepers were expected to live with their families on these two barren rocks, where even dropping in for a chat with your neighbours was complicated by their being separated by a channel 800 metres wide.

The West Tower light was never considered satisfactory and after a number of schemes to improve it came to nothing, the decision was taken in March 1903 to abandon it and to instead improve the light on the East Tower.

Three years later, it was decided to bring the families of the keepers ashore to accommodation at Ferris Point; the Maidens became a relieving station with the keepers spending 30 days at a time in the lighthouse followed by ten days serving at Ferris Point. By the 1970s plans were advanced to automate the Maidens and the dwellings at Ferris Point were demolished. By 1977 the keepers had been permanently withdrawn and the light was controlled and monitored remotely.

In the nineteenth century, the towers were the setting for a tryst worthy of a Gothic romance novel. The daughter of Hugh Redmond, the keeper at one of the lighthouses, fell in love with the assistant keeper at the other light. When weather permitted, they visited each other by boat, but the weather cannot always be relied upon to smooth the course of true love and the lovers resorted to semaphore flags for the nineteenth-century equivalent of text messaging each other across the channel. The tryst was frowned upon by both families, but, despite attempts to keep them apart, the couple eventually eloped in the dead of night and fled to nearby Carrickfergus, where they were married.

The abandoned West Tower buildings.

Chaine Tower

Location: 54° 51' 16.3" N, 5° 47' 52.7" W
Elevation: 23m
Character: Iso WR 5s
Range: 28km

The Chaine Memorial Tower in Larne is a monument erected to James Chaine, a former Member of Parliament for Antrim, who developed the short sea route to Scotland as well as establishing the town as a transatlantic port. In 1885, the great man died and legend has it that he is buried, according to his wishes, standing up and looking out to sea.

That same year, the fundraising committee sought the assistance of the Commissioners of Irish Lights to help to build and maintain a tower, but were refused. Eventually it was agreed the Memorial Committee would build the replica round tower, without a light, at Sandy Point Bay, and the Larne Harbour authority would maintain it. The approved tower was completed in January 1888. It is a

The Blackcave tunnel on the coast road.

cylindrical stone tower lighthouse with a conical roof, situated on the west side of the entrance to Larne Lough and accessed via a short causeway.

A light was ultimately installed to aid navigation off Hunter Rock, a submerged rock approximately 8 kilometres (5 miles) off shore. Converted to electricity in 1935, responsibility for maintaining the light now lies with the attending keeper at Ferris Point Lighthouse on the other side of the harbour.

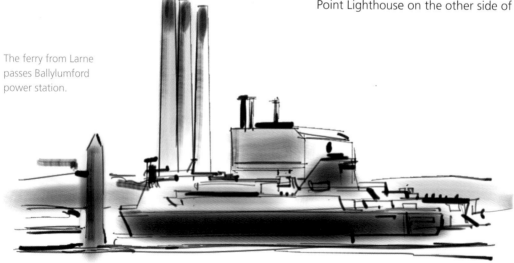

The ferry from Larne passes Ballylumford power station.

CHAINE TOWER
LIGHTHOUSE

LARNE
COUNTY ANTRIM

Ferris Point

The nearby Gobbins cliff path is a spectacular cliff-side route south to Whitehead.

Location: 54° 51' 04.5" N, 5° 47' 23.7" W

The original lighthouse at Ferris Point was finished in 1838 and the light first exhibited in 1839. It was then known as Larne Lough Lighthouse. The present building is of more recent construction but is no longer a working lighthouse – the floodlights of Larne docks are now sufficiently bright to assist ships entering or leaving the harbour. It remains, however, as a base for the maintenance of the Maidens light to the north of Larne Lough and of buoys in the vicinity. It also provides a helipad for emergency and maintenance crews.

Shipping and especially ferries have ploughed the routes between this corner of Ireland and Scotland for centuries. However, the increase in air travel has meant that routes have been cut and in late 2015 the high-speed route to Troon on the Ayreshire coast was closed, leaving Larne to serve Cairnryan as its sole route between these islands.

The old passenger ferry from Larne across to Ferris Point.

Mew Island

Location: 54° 41' 55.4" N, 5° 30' 49.4" W
Elevation: 37m
Character: Fl (4) W 30s. Exhibited by day in poor visibility
Range: 44km

The present lighthouse on Mew Island dates to the late 1800s. Prior to that there had been a cottage-style lighthouse on the nearby Lesser Copeland Island, which had an open brazier on its roof. Even before that, there had been another short-lived light on Island Magee, near Carrickfergus, also of the cottage style and one of six erected around the Irish coast by Sir Robert Reading under letters patent granted to him by Charles II.

In 1796, Thomas Rogers added a 2-metre-diameter lantern to a top corner of Copeland Island's 12-metre-tall square tower and changed the

The mighty wren.

lighting from coal to oil, using six Argand lamps. In 1810, a new 16-metre tower and lantern were built alongside the old, but as commerce into the harbour increased and Belfast became a world centre of linen, shipbuilding and rope-making, and as sailing vessels were replaced by steam-driven shipping, the merchants and shipowners began to demand a better-positioned lighthouse to guaranteed the safety of their stock. The Belfast Harbour Commissioners suggested Mew Island as the best location and work commenced in 1882 on the new station. The new light and fog signal came into operation in November 1884 with a character of 4 four-second flashes in twenty seconds repeated every minute. The 37-metre tower was constructed from stone quarried on the island and dressed with Newry granite. Until 1928, Mew Island had its own gas-making plant and remained the last of its type until 1928 when it was converted to oil. Paraffin gave way to electricity in 1969 and the station was converted to automatic operation in March 1996.

Mew Island's optic was one of the largest of its kind ever constructed, weighing 10 tonnes and measuring 7 metres tall. It is a unique heritage object with significance to Belfast's economic, maritime and industrial past and the restored light is now housed in a stunning display at the city's Titanic Quarter.

The rare and beautiful Fresnel lens from Mew Island.

MEW ISLAND
LIGHTHOUSE

COPELAND ISLANDS
COUNTY DOWN

Blackhead (Antrim)

Location:	54° 46' 01.0" N, 5° 41' 20.3" W
Elevation:	45m
Character:	Fl W 3s
Range:	50km

Only half an hour from Belfast and on the Causeway Coastal Route, Blackhead Lighthouse surveys the sea from the edge of a majestic cliff on the northern extremity of Belfast Lough and would have guided many famous vessels into and out of Belfast during its golden age of shipping, including the ill-fated *Titanic*.

This lighthouse was designed by William Douglass, the then engineer to the Commissioners of Irish lights.

The octagonal tower, standing 16 metres high, was completed in 1902 and was at the time painted red. An explosive fog signal was also added to the station. In August 1929 the decision was made to change the colour of the tower to white, presumably for reasons of visibility.

On 23 September 1965 Blackhead Lighthouse was converted to electricity and the intensity of the light was increased, giving a range of 50 kilometres.

By 1975 the light-keepers were withdrawn from the station and since then it has been in the care of a part-time attendant.

Today, Blackhead is one of twelve lighthouses that make up Great Lighthouses of Ireland, a new all-island tourism initiative offering visitors an opportunity to visit or stay in a lighthouse.

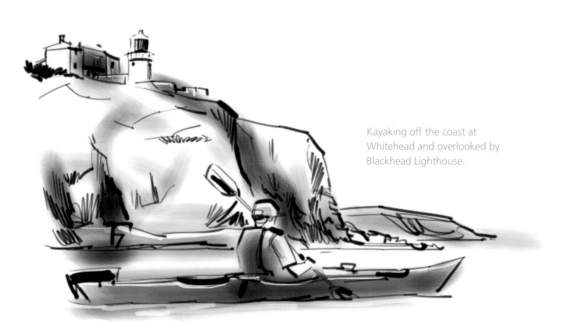

Kayaking off the coast at Whitehead and overlooked by Blackhead Lighthouse.

Donaghadee

Location: 54° 38′ 42.4″ N, 5° 31′ 51.6″ W
Elevation: 17m
Character: Iso WR 4s
Range: W: 31km; R: 24km

Looking not unlike an oversized sandcastle, the Moat, built in 1818, lords it over Donaghadee.

Donaghadee is the nearest Irish port to Scotland and in early times was the main landing point in Northern Ireland for travellers from Britain.

Trade across the Irish Sea was based on the packet service and, in 1626, a harbour was built to facilitate the boats that worked between Donaghadee and Portpatrick, only 35 kilometres away. This, however, was superseded by the Larne–Stranraer route and Donaghadee fell into decline.

The foundation stone of a new port was laid by the Marquis of Downshire on 1 August 1821. This new, improved harbour consists of two independent piers running north-westwards out to sea; parallel nearer the shore, they converge at the outer ends to form a harbour mouth 46 metres wide.

The lighthouse was established in 1836 with a fixed character, i.e. non-flashing, showing red mainly to

The *Sir Samuel Kelly* lifeboat was involved in a number of high-profile incidents, including the *Princess Victoria* tragedy of 1953 and the 1979 Fastnet Yacht race.

seaward and white over the harbour and towards Belfast Lough. The tower is built of cut limestone, fluted, and in its early days was left unpainted in its natural grey colour. Today, the tower, including the lantern and dome, is painted white with a black plinth, a decision taken sometime between 1869 and 1875.

Back at the dawn of the twentieth century, the steamship companies were in aggressive competition with each other over their various routes. In order to get their passengers to their destinations in the quickest possible time, many corners were shaved. One of these involved taking a shortcut through Donaghadee Sound instead of the longer, but safer, route around Mew Island. Three of the Belfast Steam Company's ships almost came undone as they struck a 'very hard underwater obstruction' – probably uncharted rocks – while using the sound. The marine superintendent refused to light the buoys in the sound as he reasoned it would encourage more vessels to attempt the shortcut. After his initial refusal, estimates were sought for the cost of illuminating the buoys, but it was not until three years later in 1910 that they were actually lit.

Donaghadee has the distinction of being the first Irish lighthouse to be converted to electricity, in 1934. Chaine Tower at Larne followed the next year and Tuskar in 1938.

DONAGHADEE

LIGHTHOUSE

DONAGHADEE
COUNTY DOWN

Angus Rock

Location: 54° 19' 48.0" N, 5° 31' 30.0" W
Elevation: 15m
Character: Fl R 5s
Range: 12km

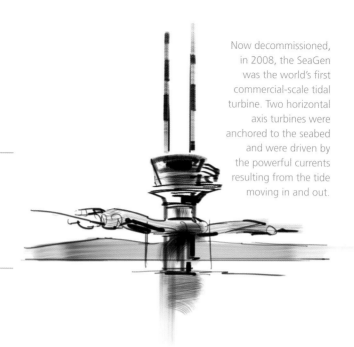

Now decommissioned, in 2008, the SeaGen was the world's first commercial-scale tidal turbine. Two horizontal axis turbines were anchored to the seabed and were driven by the powerful currents resulting from the tide moving in and out.

Angus Rock Lighthouse, or beacon, is located on a low rocky islet off the Narrows, the entrance to Strangford Lough, which boasts the fastest tidal stream in Ireland, running at up to 8 knots during spring tides The tower was built as a day mark, probably in the nineteenth century. It is mentioned as early as 1885.

Many ships have been wrecked and lives lost in and around Strangford, including *The Eagle's Wing*, the first officially recorded wreck on the Irish coast, which foundered in October 1715 near Strangford Bar with a loss of 76 lives.

Today, Strangford has little or no commercial traffic but this was not the case in the past when a considerable amount of the agricultural produce from the area around the lough was exported via sea. From the fifteenth century to the end of the nineteenth and even as recently as the 1940s,

trading schooners and ketches would have been a common sight in and around Strangford. The Angus Tower was affectionately referred to by these sailors as 'The Rocking Goose'. The nickname's origins are unclear – it probably stems from the local pronunciation of 'Rock Angus', although there is a less-popular fable that imagines the tower resembling a goose's neck – but it is still referred to by that sobriquet.

In October 1978 it was recommended to the Ballast Board that, subject to Down County Council establishing the five lights, for which they had received statutory sanction, it would approve the establishing of a light at Angus Rock Tower and, in order to complete the effective lighting of the Strangford Lough entrance, that the unlit Bar Pladdy buoy be replaced by a lighted buoy. The tower remained unlit for a considerable period of time: it was not until April 1983 that a light was eventually established on the rock.

In July 2000 the light was converted to solar power, with a character of flashing red every five seconds in hours of darkness only. It is now in the care of an attendant and monitored via a telemetry link from Irish Lights in Dun Laoghaire.

The island is noted for it seals and from it on a clear day, you can see across to the Isle of Man and the Lake District beyond.

ANGUS ROCK
LIGHTHOUSE

STRANGFORD LOUGH
COUNTY DOWN

St John's Point (Down)

Location:	54° 13' 36.3" N, 5° 39' 36.7" W
Elevation:	37m
Character:	Q (2) W 7.5s
Range:	46km

Name-checked in Van Morrison's classic song, 'Coney Island', St John's Point Lighthouse has an enviable aspect along the beautiful County Down coastline. Its strikingly tall tower is marked with vibrant bands of yellow and black. These colours, which distinguish it from other lighthouses, are known as its day mark. St John's Point Lighthouse was designed by George Halpin Senior, one of our most famous civil engineers and lighthouse builders. The light was first exhibited in 1844.

The original lighthouse was painted white and later, in 1902, three black bands were added. Its current markings of black with two yellow bands have been in place since 1954. In the early 1950s, Brendan Behan's father subcontracted the job of painting the lighthouse to his playwright son. Perhaps the colours didn't suit him. Perhaps black with a creamy white band on top might have been more his cup of tea! In any case, his work was poorly received and by

mutual consent he never reached such heights in the painting and decorating game again. The tower was originally only 14 metres tall. It was extended to its current dizzying height of 40 metres in the 1880s and is now the tallest onshore lighthouse on the Irish coast. (Fastnet is the tallest offshore lighthouse.) In 1981 the lighthouse was automated and the keepers withdrawn. A part-time attendant was appointed and took charge of the station.

Today, St John's Point is one of twelve lighthouses that make up Great Lighthouses of Ireland, a new all-island tourism initiative, and is one of eight that can be booked as holiday accommodation.

Killough Harbour.

Haulbowline

Location: 54° 01′ 11.8″ N, 6° 04′ 44.4″ W

Elevation: 32m

Character: Fl (3) W 10s. Exhibited in hours of darkness only

Range: 18km

The Vidal Bank Lighthouse.

The elegant, tapering stone tower of Haulbowline Lighthouse was built to a design of George Halpin. Originally painted white, it was restored to its natural colour in 1946. Located at the entrance to Carlingford Lough, near Cranfield Point in County Down, the fixed white light was first exhibited in September 1824 with a half-tide light displayed from the balcony halfway up the seaward side of the tower. This was lit to indicate that the tide was such that there would be enough depth for ships to pass into the lough. Until 1922, during daylight hours, a large black ball used to be hauled up on a gantry above the lantern to indicate tidal conditions, and a bell was struck by weight-driven machine every 30 seconds in foggy weather. It must have been quite spooky in the half-light for the communities along the shorelines!

The lighthouse was built on the eastern part of the Haulbowline rocks, one of a number of navigation hazards at the seaward end of Carlingford Lough. Construction of the 34-metre-high stone tower was a remarkable achievement, considering its location on a semi-submerged rock with fast currents running around it. The principal light is displayed 32 metres above sea level, with a character of flashing white three times every ten seconds.

The light was converted to electricity and made unwatched automatic on St Patrick's Day in 1965 and the fog signal was permanently disestablished on 8 January 2009.

Haulbowline occupies one of the most spectacular and romantic settings along our shores, with its diminutive Romeo-and-Juliet balcony overlooking one of Ireland's three glacial fjords (the others being Lough Swilly on the border of Donegal and Derry and Killary in Connemara).

King John's Castle overlooks the scenic harbour at Carlingford, County Louth.

HAULBOWLINE
LIGHTHOUSE

CARLINGFORD LOUGH
COUNTY DOWN

Greenore

Carlingford Ferry connects Greenore on the south
of the lough with Greencastle on the north. It's
worth taking the ride just for the scenery.

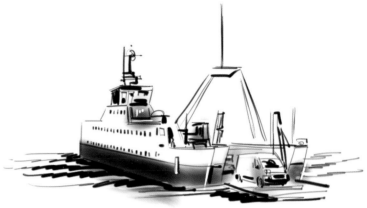

Inactive since 1986
Location: 54° 02' 01.4" N, 6° 07' 56.0" W

Built to designs by George Halpin Senior in 1830,
Greenore Lighthouse is unused and in a sorry state.
It stands a mere 11 metres tall and was built to
highlight the southern entrance of Carlingford Lough
and also Greenore Port, the only privately owned
port in the Republic. Like many harbour lights, the
array of lighting on the quayside has rendered it
redundant.

Greenore itself is situated on the southern shore of
Carlingford Lough, with spectacular views of the
Mourne Mountains to the north, and Slieve Foye
to the west. The entire village is an architectural
conservation area and contains a range of
outstanding and well-preserved Victorian residential
and industrial buildings, built by the London and
North Western Railway Company to house their port
and railway workers (the railway terminal and ferry
port was officially opened in 1873). It is reputed to
be the only completely planned village in Ireland
and at the time of its design was considered to be
state of the art.

The railway station was built inside a magnificent
hotel on the quayside, with luxury passenger
liners sailing regularly for Holyhead in Wales. A
first-class passenger could leave Euston Station in
London at 8:45 p.m. and arrive in Belfast at 9:52
a.m., including a four-hour voyage from Holyhead
to Greenore. The railway closed in 1951 with the
ferry services ceasing soon after. By 1964, the then
abandoned port was being used to fit out the ships
of the pirate radio stations Radio Caroline and Radio
Atlanta. Today, Greenore Port has seen a major
revival and thrives as conduit for the import and
export of steel, timber, feedstuffs and coal.

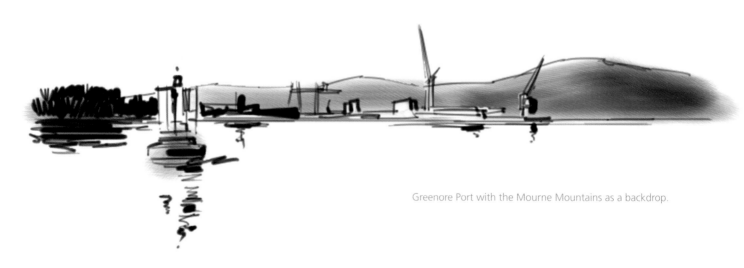

Greenore Port with the Mourne Mountains as a backdrop.

GREENORE
LIGHTHOUSE

GREENORE
COUNTY LOUTH

Dundalk

The Millennium sundial at Blackrock, County Louth. The 3-metre-high gnomon (the part which casts the shadow) is a bronze sculpture of a female diver.

Location: 53° 58′ 33.6″ N, 6° 17′ 42.8″ W
Elevation: 10m
Character: Fl WR 15s. Exhibited in hours of darkness only
Range: 18km

Dundalk Lighthouse is a screw-pile structure similar to but smaller than the one intended for, but never built, at the Kish Bank. It was established in June 1855 after a decade of correspondence requesting a light to guide the ever-increasing number of vessels into the harbour. The piles were screwed into the sand and supported a timber deck on which was placed limited wooden accommodation and a small lantern. The optic was revolved by a weight-driven machine.

The lighthouse is one of just three of its kind remaining in Ireland. The other two are at Moville and Cobh (Spitbank).

The engineering behind this unique design was pioneered by Alexander Mitchell, who, by the age of 23, was, to all intents and purposes, blind. Mitchell nevertheless refused to let his disability hamper him and pursued his vocation with a vigour and ambition that his sighted colleagues could but envy.

Based on the humble corkscrew, Mitchell's patented 'screw-pile and mooring' technique dates as far back as 1833. It ensured that the platform would not drift. The system had been proved at Maplin Sands and Belfast Lough and would be successfully employed in locations around Ireland, Britain and North America

Soon after the light was established, it was decided to add a fog-signal bell. This came into operation in November 1860. A bell was struck six times every minute by another weight-driven machine, which was wound up by the keeper on duty.

In 1989, following a hydrographic survey, the bearing of the green sector light and the day marks were adjusted to show a new channel approach line. In 2002 another survey indicated changing depths and the green sector was suspended.

Windsurfing in Dundalk Bay.

Tower of Lloyd

Location: 53° 43' 56.9" N, 6° 54' 20.2" W

'I'm looking at the river, but I'm thinking of the sea.' Randy Newsman's lyrics could have been written for the Tower of Lloyd, a lighthouse that finds itself stranded 40 kilometres from the ocean. Built in 1791, the Kells Lighthouse, as it is locally known, was never meant to steer ships to home, but instead the 30-metre-high tower was used by the Earl of Bective as a viewing platform for various country pursuits, including horse racing and the hunt, and to watch for his ships coming into Carlingford Lough to the north-east. The tower was designed by Henry

A great spangled fritillary feeding at the nearby Girley Bog Eco Walk.

Aaron Baker, who worked with James Gandon, and it was erected in the late nineteenth century by the First Earl of Bective in memory of his father, Sir Thomas Taylor. Inside there is a 164-step spiral staircase, with a central protective cage leading to the gallery on top. A plaque on the east side of the spire carries the Headfort coat of arms with the family crest 'Consequitur quodquinque petit' ('He follows what he seeks').

The spire stands on the site of an Iron Age ring fort, but it is believed that the site dates back to the Bronze Age.

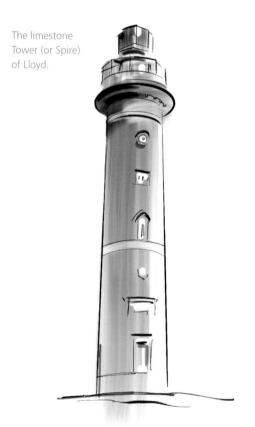

The limestone Tower (or Spire) of Lloyd.

TOWER OF LLOYD
LIGHTHOUSE

KELLS
COUNTY MEATH

Index of Lighthouses

Main entries are in bold

The Great Lighthouses of Ireland initiative comprises twelve lighthouses:

Ballycotton Lighthouse	www.greatlighthouses.com
Blackhead (Antrim) Lighthouse	www.irishlandmark.com
Clare Island Lighthouse	http://clareislandlighthouse.com/en/
Fanad Head Lighthouse	https://fanadlighthouse.com
Galley Head Lighthouse	www.irishlandmark.com
Hook Head Lighthouse	www.hookheritage.ie
Loop Head Lighthouse	www.greatlighthouses.com
Rathlin West Lighthouse	www.rspb.org.uk/rathlinisland
St John's Point (Donegal) Lighthouse	www.irishlandmark.com
St John's Point (Down) Lighthouse	www.irishlandmark.com
Valentia Island Lighthouse	www. greatlighthouses.com
Wicklow Head Lighthouse	www.greatlighthouses.com